RISE

A MEMOIR

RISE

A MEMOIR

Risé Myers

Black Bamboo Press
Los Angeles, CA

Published by Black Bamboo Press
www.blackbamboopress.com

Printed in the United States of America

Cover Design by Suzanne Nagle St. John
suzystjohn.blogspot.com

Library of Congress Control Number: 2016954841
Cataloging-in-Publication data is on file with the publisher

ISBN 978-0-9837284-1-2 (paperback)
ISBN 978-0-9837284-2-9 (ebk)
ISBN 978-0-9837284-3-6 (ebk)

To Tink
My greatest teacher, spiritual guide, and best friend.
You continue to touch my life every day.

Part I
Fall On Your Knees

WHITE GLOVES

I only have one photo of me as a young girl. I'm wearing white gloves. It had to be Easter because we never got dressed up for any other reason, but there I am in a dress and wearing white gloves, which were probably hand-me-downs. The other things in the picture are a leafless tree and our house.

I don't know if Dad was taking the photograph. But I imagine he was the one, probably wearing his fatigues and combat boots like always. I figure he was hollering at me to smile.

But I'm not smiling. Instead, my four-year-old self has on her grim face. Like I'm fighting to hold it in—what exactly, I don't know. It's not as if I had any idea that my father was about to leave us four kids and my mother and pretty much disappear to have a family with another woman. Even if I had known I wouldn't necessarily have been sad about it.

My expression probably means that, by then, I had already learned not to give too much away. To be ready for anything. It's my Cautious Face.

Here's an example of what to be ready for. A few months before Dad left, he and Mom got into one of their knock-down drag-out fights. I don't remember what it was about. It doesn't matter.

But it ended up with Mom bent over the bathtub and my father holding her head under the water with his boot. She was scratching and slapping at him, trying to get him off. We kids were standing in the doorway, blubbering and pleading. Maybe Rochelle was begging, "Daddy, please, please, don't."

Robbie snapped out of it first. He figured out to run to the neighbors to get help, and I decided to run after him. The man and the woman who lived there came charging back and pulled Dad off before Mom drowned. Then Dad started laughing. He knocked us all out of the way as he staggered out the door.

When he would finally leave for good that spring, he left us alone and with nothing. Sure, we had each other. We had our crappy furniture, dishes, some clothes. But my mother didn't know how to do anything. She had no job skills. She had been having babies since dropping out of high school at age fifteen. She didn't have any parenting skills either.

I imagine my father—handsome, disgusting, and mean—standing there on the day of the picture, holding the camera like it was a gun and he could aim it at anyone, at any time, and you'd always be surprised. I imagine him yelling, "Risé, look at the fucking camera. Stick out your hip. Pretend you're licking an ice cream." And me rigid and serious, like I was getting an award from the President.

We didn't look alike, and I'll bet I thought then that we were as different as peas and dessert, me, blond and slight in my white gloves and white dress, and him hairy and dark and wearing those giant combat boots he used to kick us around. So even though he isn't in the photo, when I look at it I can't help but think of him.

The house is sitting there and already looking empty because we were going to have to leave it as soon as he moved away.

And that poor skinny tree, reaching up like a hand to grab something out of the clouds. And nothing there in the sky to grab.

CALIFORNIA

Our home was California—Los Angeles, specifically. In 1960, California was wide open and it was growing into a primo place to live, but I didn't know any of that. The industry that started during the war was continuing to grow, and people were moving to L.A. and San Diego and building freeways and suburban housing developments. People were chasing down the jobs, the fine weather, and life among cactus plants that made you think of endless desert, and other flora, lush and flashy, that made you think you were living in an exotic jungle. All of that made you think that anything was possible, always blooming no matter what, like some kind of hope.

I didn't know that. I didn't know anything. One time, when I was older, a friend said something about snow coming early to the peaks, and I looked in the wrong direction. I didn't even know which way was the coast and which way were the San Gabriel Mountains.

All I knew about was my own family and that it wasn't right.

After the Air Force sent Dad to the Philippines, and he took some woman named Bonnie and her daughters with him like they were his real family and like we didn't exist, Mom made us pack up all of our crap and move across the street to live with a neighbor lady because we couldn't pay to stay where we were.

Mom sat in one of the neighbor lady's lawn chairs and looked at us stunned, like she couldn't believe what a disaster her life had become. Even then, she couldn't help but be pretty. She had her small mouth, v-shaped, outlined in bright red lipstick. Her dark, wide-apart almond-shaped eyes shimmered like sunlight on broken glass. Her black hair was beehived on top of her head, and some loose hair hung down, framing her triangle-shaped face, curling around under her tiny chin.

But even though she was pretty, I knew better, even by age four, than to think pretty meant nice. I already knew not to trust her, at all.

After awhile, we got on welfare and food stamps and Mom found us a crummy apartment with two bedrooms. And then she went to bed and pretty much stayed there, yelling at us to bring her a cigarette or a drink, bring her a magazine, make her a sandwich. So we four kids had to figure out how to survive.

My oldest sister, Rochelle, who was eight, sort of took charge. She scribbled the names of the different rooms on pieces of paper and threw them into a bowl. On Saturdays, we would each draw a name and that was our room to clean. But we didn't know much about cleaning so the results were lousy, dust building up in the corners, sticky prints on the walls, trash piling up in closets, mold growing along the linoleum in the bathroom.

We had cockroaches. At night when I turned on the kitchen light to get a glass of water they would scatter along the kitchen counters where we had left jars of jam open or graham cracker crumbs, baloney rinds, and used knives that had been stabbed into peanut butter.

We all scrounged for food, accepting anything that was offered to us by anyone in the neighborhood and making mixtures of cereal with powdered milk and sugar or potato chips smashed up with hot dogs on white bread.

Rochelle would try to keep us in line so we wouldn't get beat. She'd say, "Clean that up or Mom will get mad." Or "Shut your whining. You'll get us all in trouble." More often than not it didn't matter what she said or even what we did. One time, Rochelle was putting away the dishes and she dropped one. It was a plate and it just slipped out of her hand. Mom appeared in the doorway. She said, "You piece of shit. Do you think money comes out of my ass?"

I didn't know what that meant exactly or how money could do that. But then Mom grabbed Rochelle by the hair and swung her around in a circle, banging her against the kitchen counter. Rochelle showed me her bruise later.

On the weekends, if Mom dragged us with her to the grocery store with our food stamps, I knew enough, even that young, to be embarrassed. Mom with her purse clutched against her body like she didn't trust anyone, seven-year-old Robbie pushing the cart with me in it, Rochelle running up and down the aisles to fetch the things Mom would point at, and six-year-old Rhonda drifting away on her own until Mom would smack Robbie and tell him to bring her back. We were all wearing hand-me-downs and Salvation Army specials. We were dirty and loud, and I noticed people looking at us and making extra room in the aisles so we could pass by.

On our way back to the car, the sun would always be out, bouncing light off the windshields in the parking lot. I'd see a different family getting into a better car and wish they would see me in the cart and come running over. "Look at her," they would say. "She obviously doesn't belong with you. What a lovely child. Can we adopt her?" But, outside of my own head, nobody noticed. And instead we'd crowd into our station wagon, which didn't always start the first time, and Mom would fill up the car with her cigarette smoke and thwack Rochelle on her ear because two of us would be fighting in the back. "Rochelle, dammit, shut them the hell up."

Sometimes she'd reach back from the front seat and grab whatever she could—someone's hair, a knee—and she'd yank or pinch until we'd howl and then shut up, trying to swallow the sniffles so she wouldn't get mad again.

At home we'd tumble out of the car and drag the groceries into the house and put them away, shoving boxes into cabinets and bottles into the fridge. Mom would go back to bed. She'd yell, "Someone get me a drink."

I would often volunteer. I learned at a young age how to make a vodka and Coke. So I'd pop open a bottle and pour it into a glass and then add a good chug of vodka. I'd toss in some cubes from the cracked ice trays in the freezer. I'd stir it up with my finger and taste it to make sure I got it right. If I was trying extra hard and we had straws, I'd toss one in. And then I'd take it into Mom, hoping she'd notice what a good job I'd done.

One time I made the mistake of putting in a toothpick because we didn't have straws. Mom took the glass and said, "Are you an idiot? You don't use a toothpick in a drink. I could have swallowed it and died." She hurled the glass against the wall, right over my head. I never made that particular mistake again.

At night we kids would crawl into the twin beds we shared, head to toe. Some nights someone would accidentally kick someone in the head, and then a fight would break out. Mom would scream at us to shut up. We'd try and then fall back into a sweaty sleep, snoring and scratching.

I wasn't too young to notice that of the four of us lying there in the twin beds with our R names, mine was different, French-like with a little accent. Mom had picked it out for me because it was the name of a famous opera star, Risë Stevens. I found out years and years later, she got the type of accent wrong and Risë Stevens wasn't French but Norwegian-Jewish-American. She got the pronunciation wrong too, calling me Ri-say, when Stevens's name was pronounced more like Rye-ice.

Maybe Mom knew that Stevens had become the Met's leading mezzo soprano. She was the only one of the mezzos to get the attention and money usually saved for the sopranos and tenors. So she was unique, and as I grew up I imagined Mom had noticed that when she listened to the radio as a kid.

In 1958, Stevens was in the TV version of *Little Women*. She played Margaret March. In *Little Women*—I found out later—Margaret, or Meg, was the oldest daughter who wanted to live in a castle in the sky with many servants.

The main thing about Meg was that she wanted things, very nice things. Just like I did.

Getting the name of an opera star in a family of pretty regular Rs had to mean something. It had to mean that I didn't belong with the rest of them. So even though nobody at school, not even the teachers, ever knew how to pronounce my name right, and people called me Rise or teased about getting a rise out of me, I knew that the name meant something special. And even when I finally decided to change it for a few years to Risa, to save myself the trouble of having to explain, my original name still had a hold on me.

There I was, somewhere in California, this huge state that was in so many rock songs, where all the wanna-be actors and singers would land, the last frontier, warm and blooming. But in my universe, a twin bed where I was lying next to someone's feet, I thought about my name and how Mom had picked it just for me. I might be related to the others, but I knew I deserved better.

RAYMOND

When I was 18 months old, Mom got Polio. It paralyzed her and she ended up in the hospital for three months. When she came back home, she still could hardly move and just sat in a chair. She told me later how I would try to crawl on her, and she would just sit there, not moving.

I thought about that a lot when Raymond came two years after Dad left us. Raymond was Mom's baby with Bob, her new boyfriend. He was a skinny, happy baby with big ears, my own personal baby doll. I played dress up on him and shoved Cheerios into his mouth. When he was bad, I would smack him, lightly, to teach him how to behave. I carried him around on my hip and pointed at things. "That there is a spoon. That's a bottle. There's a cockroach."

We taped quarters to his ears to help them lay flat. Sometimes I would steal them, saying, "You don't need these, Baby Raymond. Your ears are fine the way they are."

Right away I noticed how he could crawl up on Mom and she'd welcome him. She'd look at him and say, "Patrick," which is what she alone called him, I don't know why. Maybe it was after her own name, Patricia. When Bob, drunk, was holding Raymond, she'd say, "Give him to me." She'd set him on her knee for a moment and then hand him back. She and Raymond looked beautiful together. Mom was glowing, her dark eyes flashing, her dark hair shining like a black halo.

I thought about the Polio and I'd put Raymond on my lap. "Baby Raymond," I would coo. "I'll buy you a horsey. Don't cry or I'll smack you." Then I would hit him, just to make the point, and he would cry.

After Raymond came, some things were better and some were worse. I didn't get a good feeling seeing him and Mom together. And sometimes I would feel a new kind of anger bubbling up inside me like a shaken can of pop. On the other hand, we all moved out of our apartment and went to live with Bob in South Redondo Beach. That house was nicer and cleaner. The toilet didn't have black lines around the bottom. The sink didn't have rust stains. There wasn't a fist hole in one of the bedroom walls.

We all liked Bob. He would say, "None of you have to go to school today." Then he would pop open a beer to celebrate and we would all cheer.

But pretty soon we had made that house just as disgusting as our old one. Rochelle would take off Raymond's dirty diaper and drop it into the toilet to soak. Then one of us other kids would come in to use the bathroom and shit right on the diaper, not noticing. Things like that.

Grandma Foote, who had come to live with us in the apartment, moved in to the new house too. Grandma was Mom's Mom. She had beautiful fingernails that she painted a bright red. It matched her lipstick. She was a big smoker, and she had scary, sparkly eyes like Mom.

She would teach us things, like "A lady never sits at the bar. She always chooses the booth." Or "A lady never smokes in public." Sometimes she would spray me with the perfume in her atomizer. She let me make her Sidecars with Tang and Whiskey or serve her Ripple wine right out of the plastic bottle.

I slept with Grandma because I was her favorite. Having her in the house meant I always had someone who liked me best. When Mom would scream at me, I'd run to Grandma and she'd say, "Oh just ignore her. She's a sourpuss crabbykins." The words didn't exactly match my mother's behavior, but they made me feel better anyway. I liked having someone who was more on my side than anyone else's. She's the one who taught me how to stash money to keep it from the others, something I still do to this day even if there's no one around to take it. At dinner she would say only to me, "You want to have fruit instead of that ice cream." I enjoyed the attention and ate only the fruit.

The one thing about Grandma that bothered me was that she didn't like Rochelle. She'd say, "Rochelle is the one who ruined your mother's life."

Evenings got calmer and we had a little more food when Mom got a job as a cocktail waitress. She would leave at six in the evening and not come home until two in the morning. While she was gone, we would break open the Oreos and Cokes and watch TV—"Ozzie and Harriet," "My Three Sons," "Bonanza," "Candid Camera," and "The Ed Sullivan Show." Raymond would crawl on the floor. I would pick him up and bounce him, sometimes a little hard. Bob and Grandma would drink. It was like we were a normal family.

I liked school that year. I had developed a crush on my Kindergarten teacher. I took every chance I got to spend recess inside, by her side, helping her make red smiling suns on the correct classwork. I helped her cut out pumpkins from orange construction paper at Halloween and snowflakes from white construction paper at Christmas. I would lie about having a cold or a stomachache so she would let me skip recess and help her. I decided that Miss Mary liked me best of all the kids in the class, and that she could see what only Grandma could: that I was special, helpful and careful.

An old couple in our neighborhood took a liking to me too. I would go over to their home after school, and they would give me Oreos and milk. At Christmas they even bought me a bicycle. My mother said I had to share it with my brothers and sisters, and in a few weeks the tires were flat and the plastic tassels that had been hanging from the handles had been pulled off. Someone had crashed it into a wall, and the white basket in the front was torn and hung like a surrender flag.

I thought Mom would get happier with the new job, but I was wrong. When she was home, she would stay in bed or she would hit us, like always, and she and Bob started having gigantic fights. She would throw things and not miss.

One day when I was six I happened to be in the bedroom with Bob and Mom, who was holding Raymond. Bob said, "Why don't you ever let me hold my own son?" Mom slapped him across the face. Then Bob did something really surprising. He pulled a pocket knife out of a dresser drawer, opened it, and stabbed himself in the chest.

I saw the blood start running down and screamed. I ran to Grandma and she called for an ambulance.

I wondered why Bob would do the work for Mom by hurting himself. Maybe he was trying to make her happy.

They took Bob away on a rolling cart, closing him in behind the ambulance doors, and we didn't see him after that. But even with him gone, the fighting continued, only now mostly between Grandma and Mom. They would scream at each other and break dishes, on purpose. One afternoon, Mom used Grandma's cane to hit her, over and over. I didn't do anything other than stand there frozen in place, unable to take my eyes off the cane, rising and falling. But Rochelle screamed for them to stop, and Grandma fell down. I guess Mom decided it wasn't worth hitting her any longer because she tossed the cane on the floor next to Grandma and left the house.

After that, Grandma started drinking earlier and earlier each day. She would pass out on the couch, and I would wake her up when I got home from school and we would talk—she would tell me stories from when she was a kid. I don't know how she did it, but even when she passed out she always made sure that her empty cocktail glass was left on a cardboard coaster and never on the table where it could make rings.

On a spring afternoon I came home and found her passed out like usual on the couch, but this time I couldn't wake her up. Her dress was hiked up over her waist, and she wasn't wearing any panties. This time her glass was tilted, partly leaning off the coaster.

Mom had already left for the day, so I ran all the way back to school and got Miss Mary. Somehow she got Grandma awake and we dragged her to the shower where Miss Mary turned on the cold water. She asked me if I knew how to make coffee. I ran to the kitchen and made it perfect, just the right amount of hot water for the heaping spoonful out of the can. I brought it back to the bathroom, careful not to spill a drop, and Miss Mary made Grandma drink it.

At my teacher conference that spring, Miss Mary said she wanted to adopt me. Mom told me when she got home. She added that she thought it was the stupidest thing she'd ever heard.

I started counting all the times someone had thought I was special and how my family had ruined it each time. Then I kicked Raymond across the back, hard, knocking him over.

SAN FRANCISCO

One day, just at the start of the summer that I was seven, Mom woke up in a lousier mood than usual. She told us to start packing our things and threw garbage bags at us to fill. She said, "You're all going to live with your father."

We found out that Mom had contacted Dad's commanding officer and turned him in. She told him all about Dad's fake family and how he had abandoned us. Dad had been forced to leave the Air Force or he would get a dishonorable discharge. So he and Bonnie and the two girls had come back to the States. But even though they'd been back for two years we still hadn't seen him.

Rochelle pleaded. "Mom, don't make us." We wailed, "Noooo." We begged and cried, but Mom wouldn't hear anything about it. "Just throw your crap in a bag," she said.

She made us get in the car and she drove us for awhile until we were in some other neighborhood that we didn't know. She pulled up in front of a house and said, "Get out. Go there."

Rochelle tried one more time. Mom said, not looking at us, "You have to go."

So Rochelle, Robbie, Rhonda, and I got out and trudged up the walkway to the front door. I looked back and Mom drove off with just Raymond.

Robbie knocked. After a moment, a man who was my father threw open the door and yelled, "Jesus Christ."

He had big dark eyebrows, like Robbie, and thick black, wavy hair. His head was square, like mine. He had a big forehead. His eyes were like two little black buttons. His mouth was wide and a little twisted, like he was worried. He was wearing a striped shirt with a collar and tan pants and gold jewelry.

There we were, his four biological children, who he hadn't seen in years, with black trash bags, standing on his front step.

Just then a cockroach crawled out of one of the bags, and Dad said, "Don't bring that shit into my house." So we went inside and left our stuff out, which Dad took right to the trash.

Living with Dad, Bonnie, and her daughters, thin little girls with glazed-over eyes, was weird. The two girls, Connie and Terry, were strange—Terry seemed just plain stupid, and they hardly talked. We didn't know anyone in the neighborhood so we had nowhere to go. Dad bought us bunk beds so we were sleeping stacked on top of each other, each one on an individual platform. I missed Grandma.

Within two weeks Rochelle and Rhonda had run away back home.

Then Dad moved Bonnie, Robbie, Connie, Terry, and me to San Francisco where he got a job as an operations manager. I had no idea what that meant. But apparently it was something to celebrate because the day we got to the new apartment with everything still packed up in the moving boxes, he and Bonnie left for the evening to go drinking.

Everything felt strange in the new place. On the ride into the city, which was all hills and no flat place to stand, the sun I had been used to seeing everywhere had, I guess, been chased off by the cold wind. Strange clouds billowed across the sky—I could see them brewing between the tall buildings that clutched at the steep sidewalks like they were afraid of sliding down.

The apartment's ceilings were too high, and the wood floors creaked under my feet.

After Dad and Bonnie left the apartment, Robbie snuck out for a few hours. I made shadow puppets on the wall to entertain the girls, using my father's desk lamp. I rummaged through the box of Bonnie's things, like her perfumes and jewelry, and I stuffed some pretty earrings into my pocket.

When Dad and Bonnie came home, they were loud and drunk. By then, Robbie and the girls were asleep in their bedrooms. I had fallen asleep on the couch. The desk lamp was still shining at the blank wall, but there were no shadows, just those of Dad and Bonnie for a moment as they walked past. I pretended I was still sleeping. If I actually had been asleep, I wouldn't have been able to hear Dad when he started beating up Bonnie in the other room.

Bonnie's daughters had pretty things, like Barbies. They had white lamps on nightstands. The shades were checkered in pink and white. The girls pulled back their hair with shiny headbands. They didn't yell or scream or throw things. Once, when I missed Rochelle and Rhonda, I shoved Connie into the side of her bed. It made me feel better.

Bonnie didn't seem to know that Robbie and I existed. One time I had to pee so badly I was banging on the bathroom door, calling out, "Please, pleeeeeease. Let me in." Bonnie didn't say a word, and she didn't open the door. I peed myself in the hall.

On my eighth birthday, Bonnie bought me a 29-cent paper doll. It was the kind with clothes that had perforated edges and tabs you folded over the doll's cardboard shoulders. I had never had a doll of my own before. But this one was junk. I threw it in the trash.

FRUITS AND VEGETABLES

I always knew what I wanted: better than what I had. I drank with my pinkie up off the plastic cup, the way Grandma did, like I was a princess. I liked clothes. I liked being clean. I wanted nice things, and I didn't like to eat vegetables.

There were certain battles I was willing to fight to get what I wanted. When I was three and a half, I refused to eat the green peas on my plate at dinner. They were lukewarm, like little hard boogers.

I crossed my arms and said, "No."

My father said, "You are going to eat every one of those goddamn peas or I'm going to cram them down your throat."

I uncrossed my arms for a second and looked at the peas. There was no way I was going to put those in my mouth and chew them. I recrossed my arms and sat back in my chair and shook my head furiously from side to side.

My father said, "You think you're too good for this food? I wonder what would happen to you if I stopped working my ass off to put supper on the table." He pointed. "Shove those into your mouth, now."

His voice was loud and harsh, but the peas were hard and awful. I kept my arms crossed and yelled, "No."

I noticed Rochelle's surprised face across the table from me. My mother said, "Oh shit," and laughed.

My father leapt up from the table like he'd been bitten by a snake. Within a second, he had grabbed the collar on my shirt and dragged me off my chair and to the floor. He said, "You think you're the boss here?" He started kicking me with his combat boots. I crawled to get away, and he kept after me, kicking me hard all the way down the hall to the bedroom. I got inside and slammed the door closed. He kicked it so hard the walls shook.

As I sniveled alone in the dark room, rubbing at the bruises that were probably already starting to blacken, I thought about how I hadn't had to eat the peas.

In San Francisco, now that I was older, Dad no longer

forced me to eat vegetables. He would shake his head in disgust and take a swig of his drink when I didn't, but that was it. Robbie, who shared my dislike, had a different strategy. He would scoop the food off his plate into his hand when he thought no one was looking. He'd go to the kitchen and dump it.

Bonnie had different rules for the girls. She would tell them they would get ice cream if they finished the broccoli or the beans. They always did. I would sneak out the ice cream later on my own and help myself to big spoonfuls of it. With each bite, I felt like I had won something. But the winning didn't feel good.

I wouldn't feel better until I had given one of the girls a kick in the leg or a cuff behind the ear. Then the jangly feeling would calm down for a while.

In the San Francisco apartment, I was regularly stealing things from Bonnie and the girls. I would take a hair ribbon and shove it into my pocket. I would grab a bottle of nail polish from the bathroom and cram it under my pillow.

Dad would leave coins on the kitchen counter when he came home from work. As soon as he started making his cocktails for the evening, the coins would disappear into the pocket of my sweatshirt.

I took a pretty postage stamp showing Johnny Appleseed, someone I had never heard of, from Bonnie's end table. This Johnny Appleseed was a bearded man carrying a shovel and a bag and walking in front of a giant red apple. He looked like some kind of hero. I decided the stamp was a sign—Johnny Appleseed was an angel on his way to save me. He would use the shovel to dig me out from my family and then give me a bite of the apple.

A FISTFUL OF COINS

Robbie and I went back to live with Mom after a few months in San Francisco. As usual, no one told us why. Dad just had us get in the car and he drove us back to Los Angeles and to a new place where Mom, Rochelle, Rhonda, and Raymond were living. He said, "Alright then. Don't be strangers." He swatted Robbie on his butt and he air kissed me in the general area of my hair.

Mom was at work when we arrived. As soon as I got inside, Rochelle and Rhonda took me into what turned out to be our bedroom, a small square space with two beds, one window, and piles of stuff on the floor. "Mom's pregnant," they both said at the same time as we all plopped down on one of the beds.

Rochelle said, "His name is Henry. We met him once."

"Who?" I didn't understand a thing.

"The father."

There was another father. That made three so far.

Rhonda said, "Mom tried to give Raymond away when we were gone at Dad's." Now that was surprising. I had figured she had kicked us out so she could be alone with Raymond. That news made me feel a little happy.

Rochelle said, "She picked him back up a couple of days later."

Rhonda said, "She had to get a lawyer."

This was a lot of information for me to take in, and I wasn't sure what a lawyer was. I stared dully at the floor. I remembered what had happened when Raymond was born, and I wondered if we would be going back to live with Dad when the new baby came.

Nothing made any sense. Now I was back home, but it was a different home, and this Henry they mentioned, someone I didn't even know, was probably part of it.

When my sisters left the room, I tried to hide my bag of things under one of the beds to keep something just mine and safe, but Rhonda found it in about ten minutes and put on one of my shirts. She had found the stolen coins too. "What's this from?"

"Give it back," I yelled and tried to grab the money out of her fists.

"Was Dad giving you money or did you steal it?"

I lunged at her, and she danced away. "That isn't fair, you know. You should share it with us."

As Rhonda divided up my money into three piles, Rochelle interrupted, "How was San Francisco?"

I shrugged. "It's got a lot of hills," I said. "And wind." I punched Rhonda in the shoulder. She was small, a lot smaller than Rochelle, but I was surprised by how strong she was when she jumped on top of me and pulled my hair.

I felt sick to my stomach, and the pain didn't get better until a few minutes later when I walked on purpose into Raymond, knocking him against the back of a chair.

That first night, after Rhonda and Rochelle were asleep, I crawled out of bed and found my coins where they had each hidden them. I found an even better hiding place for them, inside the rubber doorstopper that was rammed under the closet door, which no one ever shut, and once in bed again I fell back quickly into a heavy sleep.

The next day when Mom saw me and Robbie, she gave us a sideways smile and said, "So you're back in the circus." I offered to make her a drink, and she accepted.

My new life back in L.A. was about school, finding food, and trying to keep Mom happy. I did as many things as I could think of to please her, and maybe she hit me a little less than the others. But then I would let my guard down and forget to bring her her cigarettes, for example, and she would cuff me.

I spent my free time trying to earn money or watching old Doris Day movies, which I loved, at the Park Theater in Gardena, for 35 cents. One of my favorites was *That Touch of Mink* in which Doris Day's working-class character gets courted by the wealthy Cary Grant character. He just wants to have an affair, but she wants to get married. In the end she wins, and they do get married, but Cary Grant develops a nervous rash in a charming way.

I also loved *April in Paris*, with Ray Bolger, who plays a statesman. Because of a misunderstanding, Day's chorus girl character gets invited as the representative of American Theater to a Paris art exposition instead of the similarly named well-known stage actress. She and the statesman fall in love.

My plan was somehow to woo a wealthy statesman and become the perfect wife. I would starch my husband's shirts. I would pack healthy lunches in brown paper bags for our two children. I would wear fine, classic clothes, like pantsuits. I wasn't sure exactly how I would get there, but I knew what I wanted.

JUSTICE

The best thing about third grade was Brian Cunningham, my first love. I wanted to marry him for two reasons. One, he wore a watch, which made him look smart and mature. Two, his father was a minister.

I would sit and daydream about being a minister's wife. When "Son of a Preacher Man" by Dusty Springfield came on the radio, I would sing along. In 1966, girls couldn't even wear pants to school so being a minister's wife was the extent of my dreams at the time.

Mrs. Fraser was my third grade teacher. I tried to win

her over, but she was as hard as glass. I'd offer to spend recess with her, and she'd say, "Risé, get outside with your classmates." I'd jump up to close the classroom door after everyone came back in from recess, and she'd say, "Risé, sit down. I didn't give you permission to stand."

One thing was, she knew how to pronounce my name.

When I would hit a classmate, Mrs. Fraser always found out, and she'd send me to the principal. I would have to wait outside his office on the hard wooden bench in the hall. While I waited I would fidget and chew on my nails, dreading the beating I'd get later from Mom.

But Principal Winston had a way of calming me down. His voice was soft and he never seemed to get too worked up about my hitting problem.

"Risay," he would say, "do you think it would be possible for you to refrain from hitting the other boys and girls?"

He was so nice about it, I always vowed to give it a try.

But if he called my Mom to let her know what had happened or, worse, made her come in to talk about it, I would get a good beating at home. And that would always make it really hard for me to "refrain from hitting the other boys and girls" the next day at school.

Steven was a short, fat kid with a crewcut in my class. One day, soon after my promise to Principal Winston, when we were lining up outside for roll call, he slugged me in the back. I bit my lip and held my breath. I tried counting to ten and then I extended the count to twenty.

We marched into class and sat down. Mrs. Fraser started writing the next assignment on the chalkboard. I jumped out of my seat because my fury was like rocket fuel. Steven's eyes looked a little worried, but he forced himself to hold a rigid smirk on his fat mouth.

I said in my calmest voice, which was somewhere between an outside voice and an outright yell, "Mrs. Frasier."

She didn't turn around. So I increased the volume: "Mrs. Frasier." I added, "Steven hit me," and I saw that now Steven truly did look worried. Mrs. Frasier turned her head, for a second, but then continued writing.

So I cranked the volume and hollered, "AREN'T YOU GOING TO PUNISH HIM?"

I couldn't believe it when I got sent to the principal's office again. Principal Winston said, kindly, "Risé, do you think you might be able to confine your volume to an appropriate speaking level?"

At recess I kicked Steven in the balls.

L.A. TIMES

It turned out that Henry, who was only twenty-three, already had two kids of his own, Henry and Lisa. They were about five and three when we first met them. To avoid the obvious confusion with the two Henry names, we started calling the older one Big Henry.

But he wasn't big. He was medium size, quiet and gentle. He had broad shoulders, which made him seem strong and solid. His hair was the same color as mine. We all loved him and his gentle blue eyes right away, and his poor kids had to compete with the five of us for his attention.

He never got mad at us, and when Mom did, he would try to calm her down. Even though it rarely worked, we appreciated the effort.

When Big Henry and his kids moved in, home was even more crowded than ever before, with us girls packed into twin beds in one room and the boys packed into their beds in another. Mom and Big Henry shared the bigger room down the hall. When Renee was born, I was sure the old filthy house was just going to burst from too many people, sending clouds of dirt and stink sky high into the night air.

But it didn't, and instead Henry and Mom broke up a year later, and we needed money again without Big Henry's body and fender shop salary. Mom's waitressing job didn't bring in enough so we got back on welfare. And we all got a paper route.

On our delivery days we would wake up at 3 a.m. Mom or Rochelle would drive us all—Robbie, Rhonda, Raymond, me, and baby Renee—in our Ford station wagon to the Olympic printing plant downtown where they made the L.A. Times. The plant was enormous, like a mall parking garage for giant rolls of paper, and full of whirring and chugging machines. I would try to block out the sound by plastering my hands over my ears, but it would get inside anyway and leave me feeling numb.

At the plant all of us, except for Raymond and Renee because they were too young, would fold the papers and feed them into a machine that would tie a string around each one. I imagined robotic hands inside carefully crossing the strings, making a loop, looping another loop around it, and then pulling the ends tight. The paper bundles would shoot out, perfectly tied, like little inky pillows. We would gather them into a big basket on wheels and push them out to the car.

Then we would set out to deliver the papers. We'd finish up just around 6 a.m. when it was time to get ready for school.

In my fourth-grade class I would fall asleep, almost every day. I still missed Miss Mary from kindergarten, but Mrs. Kim was starting to win me over. When I would fall asleep, she wouldn't get mad at me. Instead, she would send me to the school nurse's office, where I would be allowed to take a nap, and get the whole bed to myself.

The nurse wanted to know why I was so sleepy all the time. I told her about the paper route, and somehow the news got back to Mrs. Kim who decided that going to church was just what I needed.

So on Wednesday nights and Sunday mornings, she and her husband would drive to our neighborhood to pick me up. I lied and told them I lived three doors down so they wouldn't see our real home. I would wait outside the neighbors' house until the Kims drove up and then, wearing my best used clothes, I'd smile and climb into the back seat of their Lincoln.

Church was what I thought heaven might be like: full of gold chandeliers and stained glass windows. Everything was very organized, with the hard wooden benches set up at equal intervals. Incense that smelled like some kind of spicy food wafted throughout the nave of the church. I would take huge gulps of it to store in my lungs for when I got back home again. Large green silky banners hung down from the ceiling. The pastor wore a dark well-ironed suit.

The pastor said all kinds of things I didn't understand, but what I did get was that this was a place where things were calm and orderly and pretty. If God wanted us to believe in him, this is how he would bribe us. I eagerly said yes.

Mrs. Kim played the organ up on a balcony, sending out thundering waves of what sounded like angel marching music, the sound that would accompany you on your climb up the golden staircase to heaven. On my climb, I would be wearing a white dress, silk gloves, and a gold tiara. My mother would be staring at me, shaking her head, with a little twist of jealousy in the corner of her mouth. My father would be hollering at me to smile in between sips from his drink, and all my brothers and sisters, as I left them behind, would see how I had been the good one all along, clearly cut from a better fabric.

In church, I would fall asleep against Mr. Kim's shoulder. His wife was right. This was exactly what a young, tired girl needed.

THE HOSE

Big Henry and Mom made up and the house got crowded again. They tried to make us a normal family. They gave us a small allowance, so we all did small things to make our home organized. Rochelle had us put our stuff in different cardboard boxes instead of in piles on the floor. Robbie threw out the empty Weldwood contact cement glue jars in his room. Mom even put a chore list on the fridge, and for a few months, we occasionally made check marks on it.

But, over time, we all slipped back into our chaotic patterns. Robbie shot out one of the windows with a BB gun, and Mom clobbered him on the head with her fist. "You're paying for that."

When I came home late from the park, Mom hollered from the bedroom, "Where the hell have you been?" I brought her a drink, but got too close to the bed and she managed to cuff me on the chin. "Don't think you're better than me," she hissed.

She got into a battle with Rochelle one day when dinner was late. Big Henry said, "Honey, we're lucky we've got someone to make dinner." Mom kicked him in the shin and then went after Rochelle with a spatula. She slapped her across the back of the head about seven times before Big Henry could grab a hold of her hand.

One night Mom and Big Henry had friends over for drinks. They told us to stay in our rooms, but we kept sneaking out to spy on the grownups. Rochelle brought almost-empty glasses of booze back to our room so we could drink them. We were spying when some blond woman made the stupid mistake of sitting on Big Henry's lap. Mom grabbed a butcher knife from the kitchen and charged the woman. It took four men to hold her down. Big Henry then picked her up and carried her toward the front door. On the way out, she kicked out a window and cut up her leg and had to go to the hospital.

Another time I got caught for stealing money from Mom's purse. She wanted to get a piece of me. But Big

Henry said, "No. I'll do it," something he'd never offered before. I watched through the window as he went outside and cut a section off the garden hose with his knife, leaving the rest of the hose useless and nonfunctional, like a dead snake. When he came back in he told me to hold on to the back of a kitchen chair. He wouldn't look at me. I tensed up, holding on, and he gave me five lashes with the hose across my shoulders.

I cringed and sobbed, gripping the back of the chair. The lashes left me swollen and black and blue all across my upper back. But even worse was the fact that Big Henry wouldn't look at me, even when he gently put a bag of frozen peas across my shoulders.

But Mom did look at me, after. She came to the bedroom door and watched me crumpled up on the bed as I was trying to muffle my sobs into my thin pillow. I eventually dragged myself up to look at her and I glared back defiant and self-righteous. She had long ago lost all the muscles in her neck from the Polio, and as she often did she was holding up her head with a hand elegantly posed under her chin.

She said, "You dirty rotten mother fucking son of a bitch. You'll never amount to anything."

Mom always wore turtlenecks to hide the damage to her neck. That night, she was dressed in a black one and a classy blazer with gold buttons, and even though she had just strung a series of awful words together, I thought she looked like she had just stepped off a movie set, maybe for a movie in which Doris Day is an angry brunette directing a gang of thugs to kick a rash-stricken Cary Grant unconscious.

I hated her just the same.

That night I got hit twice. The first was the sting of having Big Henry volunteer for the job. Obviously, he thought I was a good-for-nothing criminal, and I was ashamed. The second was Mom knowing exactly the worse thing she could say to me, because amounting to something was what I wanted more than anything in the world.

I cried ugly, spiteful tears after Mom left. "I am better, I am better," I said over and over again to myself. What I meant was that I was better than they were. The reason I had to say it so much was that I was having trouble convincing myself—how was I any better when I had acted just like they had, stealing from Mom's purse? To help, I made lists in my head of the people who thought I was special: Mrs. Kim, Miss Mary, Grandma, and, formerly, Big Henry. But now Big Henry had seen the truth: That I would never amount to anything.

I was full of pathetic self-pity and furious self-hatred. But by the time I was done crying, I had decided that I had to change my life somehow.

HUNGER

As I got bigger and older, it seemed like I got hungrier too. Mrs. Kim invited me to her house for dinner. I gobbled up the meat loaf and mashed potatoes and even had a few bites of peas, which were far different from any I had had before, soft, juicy, and almost good.

The Kims didn't have any kids of their own, so I got to be their kid that night. I made sure my manners were perfect, carefully laying the cloth napkin back on the table each time after dabbing my mouth and setting my fork back down beside my plate after every bite, two mistakes that at the time I was sure were perfect behaviors.

Mr. Kim poured me two glasses of milk, one right after the other, and for dessert we had cherry pie, which dissolved in my mouth and ran down my throat into my eager belly. The cherries were tart, a word I hadn't learned yet and couldn't use, the crust was flaky and buttery, but I couldn't have described it that way then.

After helping with clean up, I followed Mrs. Kim down her carpeted hall to her bedroom. I sat on their high puffy bed as Mrs. Kim showed me a book she kept on her nightstand, *The Bible*, bound in leather with the words hammered into the skin in gold.

I felt the book but didn't read a word. The weight was all I needed. I could tell that this book contained answers. I didn't want to read it—it was too long—but I did want to talk to the author somehow.

Then Mrs. Kim showed me her closet, which was full of suits and dresses. On the top shelf there was a row of wigs in different colors, each one on its own faceless Styrofoam head, the wigs arranged from pink to red to brown to black to blue.

That was what it was like at the Kims.

At home, on the other hand, we battled over the ripped-open bag of chips and guzzled sodas. Big Henry sometimes brought us a bag of pretzels, and we savaged it, chomping down on the salty, crunchy twists, sending crumbs flying in different directions.

Rochelle would stir Hamburger Helper into a glob of discounted ground beef, and I would claw at the salty mush and hook an uncooked handful into my mouth before she could hit me with the spoon.

Renee sucked on her bottle of formula all the time. Robbie chugged Mom's alcohol and sniffed from his glue jars. I hoarded candy—whatever I could get my hands on—taking little nibbles to make it last as long as I could and rehiding it under the mattress. Rhonda shoplifted beer and cigarettes—she was wild and got into trouble constantly. Rochelle puffed on pilfered cigarettes like they were little tubes of emergency oxygen.

My mother would come home and call for a vodka and Coke if it was afternoon or plain coffee if it was morning. One time I watched her eat an entire Hershey's bar. She didn't offer a single bite to anyone.

Despite the hunger, when I became a Girl Scout in fifth grade I left the cookie boxes intact. This was an enterprise, I understood, and the boxes represented advancement. No matter how hungry I was, the boxes would stay sealed. They were for sale only.

I had to walk about a mile to get to the weekly meetings. Since we couldn't afford the green uniform and sash, the scout leader altered a used one to fit my scrawny seventy-five pounds. It still sagged on me, but

I wore it proudly each week on my long walk.

That year I sold more cookies than all of my fellow troopers. The day I found out about the honor, I let my brothers and sisters battle it out over the hot dog and pasta salad we had for dinner. I would wait my turn. I could afford to because I was a top seller.

SIPHONS

Following my Girl Scout success, I decided I liked business and was good at it. So when Robbie approached Rochelle, Rhonda, and me with a money-making plan, I signed on.

Robbie explained that our paper route was a potential gold mine. "Look, guys, when we go to collect from people, I'll case the joint. Then we hide in the bushes until they go out. We know they pay for a paper route, so they've got to have money."

It made sense. So we went to work. Rochelle and Rhonda and I would walk up the front steps of a customer's home and knock, looking as innocent as we could. "Hi. We're here to collect for paper delivery," we would say. Meanwhile, Robbie would sneak around back and peer into windows and through sliding glass doors to see what the situation was.

The customer would pay us. We would thank them fake sweetly and then reconvene with Robbie under a hedge. "So there's a purse on the kitchen counter, and in the bedroom there's a big jewelry box."

When the people left their home to go shopping or whatever, we would slip around back and Robbie would pry open the sliding door with a screwdriver or slice the window screen with a butter knife and roll it back so Rhonda could crawl through. She would let us in. Then we would run around grabbing whatever we could—loose change, jewelry, snacks, silver candlesticks—and re-emerge around the front of the house, everything stuffed into our pants and sleeves, walking fast down the sidewalk.

One time, Robbie draped a towel over a TV set and lugged it down the street away from our victims' house. Nobody seemed to notice what we were up to, so we kept at it.

The problem was figuring out how to convert our thievery into cash since no one in a pawn shop would deal with us kids. Rochelle came up with the idea of asking Mom for help. After we snagged some diamond rings from a lady's home, Rochelle told Mom she had found them in the school bathroom. Mom agreed to take them to the pawn shop down the street.

Our victim reported the theft to the police who went right to the local pawn shop and found the rings there. It wasn't hard for the police to make the connection to us. That's when Robbie, as the ringleader, was taken for the first time to Juvenile Hall. Mom said to the police, "The brats lied to me."

We siphoned gas, too, from our neighbors. After it got dark, we would sneak next door with a piece of rubber hose. Robbie would pry open the gas tank door and unscrew the cap. Then Rochelle, Rhonda, and I would take turns sucking on the hose until we got enough gas into it for Robbie to divert it into a bucket.

I never thought about whether what we were doing was wrong. I just figured those people had more than we did, and we needed help badly, so it made sense for us to redistribute the goods more fairly. It wasn't like we were being lazy—to the contrary, we were working very hard to get what we took. I even lied to myself that my troop leader would be proud of my enterprising nature.

The stealing happened among family too. After Dad and Bonnie moved back to L.A., I would visit them sometimes. At some point during the visit, I would sneak one of the girls' dolls into my sweatshirt. But when it was time to go back home, Bonnie would check me at the door and make me hand over whatever I had stolen.

She was like a brick wall in my way.

Following the newspaper route theft fiasco, I started an ironing handkerchiefs business, charging five cents per handkerchief. One time I sizzled the back of my hand against the hot iron by mistake. For weeks after I would look at the scar when I was bored in class, and it made me feel proud. It was like a tattoo of my industry.

I then got a job at the local pharmacy, cleaning the shelves for fifty cents an hour. I also started babysitting for neighborhood families, telling the parents that I wouldn't watch their kids unless I was allowed to hit them when they misbehaved.

I guess my hard work started showing because once, when Big Henry and Mom had friends over for drinks, one of their friends pulled me aside when she was on her way to the bathroom. "Ri-zee," she said, mispronouncing my name, "I see something in you, honey. You're going to be a big deal someday."

I sucked that up and held on to it for weeks.

SURPRISE

I liked gifts, but I didn't like surprises.

For a while, life settled into a sort of rhythm. Big Henry and Mom got married. Grandma moved out and got her own place and a job waitressing at the Five and Dime lunch counter—I had been seeing her less anyway because of all my jobs. She was less fun than she used to be, drinking more and falling asleep earlier and earlier. Mom and Big Henry would fight a lot but they got along too, and Big Henry made things calmer. Henry and Lisa were grown up a little more and could talk and hit back.

Raymond was no longer a toddler and he started helping us with our money-making plans. Robbie had come home again from Juvenile Hall.

By the time I was in sixth grade Rochelle and Robbie were going to the junior high school, so in the morning they would head off in a different direction. The rest of us would walk to school in a clump and then go to our various classrooms, like scattering insects. My teacher, Ms. Beatty, was nice enough, and I tried to make her like me by offering to help her at lunch, but she usually didn't have anything for me to do and encouraged me to hang out with the other kids.

After school, we all did different things—for me it was my jobs. All the money I made I kept squirreling in different places around the house, hoping that none of my siblings would ever find it. I checked on it often, like it was eggs waiting to be hatched.

As usual, our house was noisy, chaotic, and full of people. I always looked forward to nighttime because then a sort of quiet would fall on everything. Except for the occasional battle over bed space or trip to the bathroom or kitchen for water, we were still. A car would rumble by outside, but that only made the stillness inside more noticeable. It was a gift that was just mine.

Sometimes I could hear mice scurrying across the roof. The fridge motor would start humming. The toilet would be running quietly. Some sister would sigh or snore softly.

But those sounds were known and soothing. The only one awake, I would pray to the god of Mrs. Kim's church. "God, thank you for the quiet. Thank you for my money." I would also throw in some prayer that I had memorized:

He heals the brokenhearted,
and binds up their wounds.
He determines the number of the stars;
he gives to all of them their names.
Great is our Lord, and abundant in power;
his understanding is beyond measure.
The Lord lifts up the downtrodden;
he casts the wicked to the ground.

I always went over the wicked part fast so I didn't have to think about it too much. It bothered me, the thought that I might be a little wicked and could be cast down.

One night, though, I was surprised.

I was twelve years old, lying awake in bed, next to Rhonda's legs. Suddenly, I felt the sheet lift up and a warm hand touch my arm. Then the hand moved to my belly. At first I thought it might just be Rhonda turning over, but in the dark I could make out Robbie's head. "Risé," he whispered. "Risé."

I pretended to be asleep and said nothing. Robbie moved his hand to my shorts and started inching his fingers down into my panties. "Risé," he hissed. I lurched, but clenched my teeth and squeezed my eyes shut.

Robbie then carefully crawled over Rhonda's legs into the slim space left on the bed. He took my hand and put it on his penis, which was hard and sticking out from his boxers. It felt like a clump of raw hamburger. "Risé, please rub it. Risé."

I was frozen into a horrified fake sleep, apparently the deepest sleep anyone had ever achieved without being comatose. I said nothing and lay still as Robbie pumped his penis into my thigh, touching me beneath my panties.

He then left quietly.

I continued to lie frozen in place as if maybe it hadn't happened and I was going to wake up at any moment. But daylight eventually came, harsh and slanted through our one window, and I was still awake.

PRAYER

I continued my nighttime praying, but I had stopped thanking God for things. Now I was focused on asking.

"Please, God, pleeeease," I would say, putting my effort into the length of syllables instead of the content of my entreaties. "Pleeeeease don't let him come to my bed tonight."

Sometimes it worked and sometimes it didn't, which made me feel (a) like God wasn't listening all that carefully, (b) like God wasn't listening at all and Robbie's appearances were just random, or (c) like God was a mean bastard who was torturing me. I assumed that Robbie would figure out—he had to—that I didn't want him to come into my bed, and since he cared about me he would stop. But that didn't happen. And I didn't say anything.

The fact that I didn't made me mad at myself. I hissed, "Stupid" and "Coward" over and over to myself in the bathroom, on the bus, as I walked down the sidewalk. I was filled with self-hatred and I took it out on whoever was near by—except Robbie. I slugged Raymond in the shoulder. I tripped Renee and laughed when she fell. I pinched the backs of Rochelle's thighs.

Every night that he'd creep under the covers, I'd hold my breath for long stretches and pretend I was asleep. I'd listen for the sounds of my sisters—were they dreaming? Couldn't they hear what was going on? Robbie would pray into my ear like I would pray to God, "Pleeeease, Risé," he'd say, "pleeease," and, like God, I wouldn't answer.

He started saying, "Risé, I'll pay you," which wasn't an entirely bad idea since money was a big motivator for me. He left money under my pillow the way the Kims would toss a dollar into the basket at church. But just like with the money in the basket, as much as I wanted it, I never touched it.

During the day, I was so exhausted from my nighttime vigils I would fall asleep in class. My teachers didn't notice—it was probably a relief since then I was one less kid to bother with. I would fall asleep at dinner. My mother would slap the table with her hand and then shoot me a mean look, but she didn't ask why. Big Henry would tease me: "Rough night?" He would wink and smile.

Robbie wouldn't look at me. I wouldn't look at him. We were suddenly strangers. Our physical closeness at night wrenched us apart in daylight.

I quit my pharmacy job. I stopped stealing too. After school I would fall asleep on the couch, next to Big Henry drinking or Rhonda smoking or Raymond turning the pages of a superhero comic book. Days were an endless stretch of worried time and jumbled thoughts. Nights were a mean span of terror and a groping for the salvation of daylight when I would drag myself from the bed and stumble into my clothes and trudge off to school.

One afternoon, Rochelle offered me a sip of her beer, and I took it. Even though beer had always tasted funny to me, like a skunk might, I wanted the warm feeling I would get in my stomach, just like crawling under a blanket, one that no one else could crawl under with me. That with a few hot puffs from Rhonda's cigarette and I could get through the hours until bedtime.

Another afternoon Rochelle said, "Something's going on with you." But Mom yelled from her bedroom, "Someone do the goddam laundry." So Rochelle lumbered off the couch and left me with the bottle of beer.

The house reeked of cigarettes and old stale beer, rotting food, and unwashed clothes. We all perched on the furniture like a flock of crows waiting our turn at the carcass, cawing and hoping for something, anything, to happen. Rochelle blasted "Born to Be Wild" on her transistor. In her bedroom Mom read novels. Big Henry sat in his large chair and watched football. Rhonda danced on the coffee table, wagging her hips, and howling, "Baby Won't You Light My Fire," which made Mom mad and yell back for us to shut up. Renee, who was four, locked herself in the bathroom and smeared Mom's makeup on her face. Henry and Lisa fought over their few, crummy, hand-me-down toys.

Sometimes I would make dinner for everybody in an effort to make things different. I shopped for the groceries and then unpacked them all on the counter. One time it was a hamburger lasagna and garlic bread. I layered the noodles and the cheeses and the burger meat carefully and got it all in the oven. Then I needed a drink. I forgot to get the bread started. By the time I served everything, the lasagna was cold. The garlic bread came out when everybody was just about done, which, in my defense, only took about five minutes.

My mother said, "Jesus. It might have been good if it had been served at the same time. But it's fucking ice cold."

Big Henry said, "If you don't have anything good to say, don't say anything at all."

Mom rolled her eyes.

Everybody had friends over all the time. We'd all sit around and drink and smoke. Some days there were sixteen kids in the house, in the yard, on the porch.

Sometimes Rochelle and her boyfriend, a man who worked as a barber, would disappear into a bedroom. Rhonda would come home late, crawling through the bedroom window stinking of cigarettes. Robbie and a girl would disappear into the garage. I wondered why that girl wasn't enough for him. I heard Big Henry yelling at Rhonda one morning about where she had been all night. She yelled back, "Don't worry. He doesn't want nothing from me. He's married." Big Henry had to spank her with the hose for that.

Everybody was always talking and making a racket, smoking, drinking, lighting things on fire. There were bags of downers and uppers on the coffee table. People were necking on the couch. Someone was throwing up in the bathroom. The sheets on the beds stank. Underwear and socks gathered like dust bunnies along the baseboards. I had nervous hands, bouncing all over the place like newly hatched spiders looking for a place to settle.

At night I'd press those hands together, the way I'd seen Mr. Kim do in church. "God, I'll make a deal with you. Whatever you want, just get me out of here." But there was never an answer.

A HOLE IN THE HEART

Renee was born with a hole in her heart. When I was twelve and she was four, we found out she needed to have surgery and there was a fifty percent chance she wouldn't make it.

On the day before the surgery, Mom gave Raymond, Henry, and Lisa solid beatings, and Big Henry had to get involved, saying that the kids were "upset too." Mom punched him in the shoulder for that. The next morning, we all clambered into the station wagon and drove to the hospital, Renee earning the special spot on the front seat between Mom and Big Henry. At the hospital, we gathered in a large waiting room filled with plastic chairs, taking up a whole row. Everyone gave Renee a hug goodbye, just in case.

During the surgery, Robbie stayed at the opposite end of the row of chairs from me. Mom paced and smoked. Rhonda had snuck in a bottle of rum, and we took turns swigging from it. Henry told the nurses that the candy machine had eaten his money, convincing them to give him a refund, which he used to get a Snickers bar. Rochelle started flirting with a male nurse. She told us he was a doctor, but the doctors wore white coats so I knew she was wrong.

A woman in the waiting room gave us a sneering look and made the *tsk* sound while she read from a magazine. When she got up and walked past us, Robbie made sure to stick out his leg, and she fell over it, hard, onto her knees, hooting like an old bird on the way down. The nurses trotted over and gathered around her. She glared at us. "They did it," she said. The nurses looked, and Robbie jumped up out of his seat and said, "Ma'am, may I offer you a hand? Looks like you took a bad fall." She accepted, and he helped hoist her up. I had never heard him speak like that before. I didn't know what impressed me more: that he had tripped her or that he could cover his tracks so well.

I remembered for a minute that I hadn't always been afraid of him, and I couldn't help but snicker.

After about five swigs from Rhonda's bottle, I got sleepy and dozed off in my plastic chair, leaning against Rochelle's shoulder. When I woke up, Big Henry and Mom were talking to a man in a white coat. Rhonda leaned over toward me from her chair. "Renee made it," she said.

Renee had beaten the odds. I had forgotten to pray for her, but maybe this was a sign that things weren't all going to hell. Mom, who was wearing a checked blazer with gold buttons and navy wide-bottom pants, was holding her neck with one hand while she talked to the doctor. She patted her belly with the other like it was the rump of a new baby. Her eyes glittered.

My head hurt, but I felt good for the first time in months. Renee would live. Robbie was still my brother and had taken care of that old bitch. Here we were all of us gathered together when one of us was in trouble. Big Henry came over and said we were all going out for ice cream cones. We jumped up excitedly, Renee temporarily forgotten, and trotted toward the door. Suddenly, Mom smacked me on the back of the head. "Don't drink if you can't hold your liquor," she said.

FAIL

During that sixth-grade year at Washington Elementary, my grades, which had never been very good, took a dive. I guess it was because of all the things that had been happening. But also because of all the things that had been happening, I wasn't even aware of the dive.

I found out one day when Ms. Beatty turned down the lights to show us a film. It was about Dr. Martin Luther King Jr. who had recently been assassinated for fighting for civil rights. During the movie she called each one of us up to her desk one at a time to get our midyear grade. When it was my turn, I peered through the dark at her gradebook and saw an F.

"Doesn't F mean you didn't even try?" I asked.

Ms. Beatty said, "An F, honey, means you weren't good enough."

I burst into tears, grateful for the low lights so none of my classmates could see. I slumped back to my seat and wiped my eyes with the bottom of my shirt. In the movie, which had gone all blurry because of the tears in my eyes, a man was saying, "We must remember that intelligence is not enough. Intelligence plus character—that is the goal of true education."

I guessed I just wasn't smart enough for my education to give me intelligence. Through my teary eyes I watched thousands of black people standing together and listening to Dr. King make a speech. That was a lot of people agreeing about civil rights. I looked around and some kids were drawing, one kid was picking his nose, two girls were whispering. I was crying by myself in the dark classroom.

That was the day I gave up on education. Officially I kept going to school, but I skipped classes all the time, and no one even noticed.

I decided if I couldn't have intelligence or character, I was at least going to have money. In all my new free time I got back to work again. Rhonda was sleeping with the married manager of a nearby Jack in the Box.

When I turned thirteen, after I got myself a fake ID, she convinced him to hire me. I would stand on the corner of Sepulveda and Cabrillo, wearing the Jack in the Box head sphere on my scrawny, undeveloped body, and wave at people driving by.

After that I got a better paying job—$1.35 an hour—working at the Der Wienerschnitzel in Redondo Beach. I kept working there for a year until the boss caught me stealing from the register. Making money was going too slowly, and taking extra from the cash drawer would speed up my plan. But being fired made me lose the rest of my confidence. I started feeling hopeless. I wasn't smart enough to do well in school, and I couldn't even keep a job. What could I expect from the future? I needed a new strategy.

CAMP HAWTHORNE

Robbie continued making nighttime visits to my bed, not every night but just enough that every night I would lie still and terrified, unable to sleep. But every time he crawled into bed, I would pretend to be asleep. And when he left, I would lie awake, my eyes open but unseeing.

This new part of my life made everything else duller and flatter. When something good happened, like Big Henry brought home a pizza or I went to visit Grandma, it didn't feel as good as it would have before. It was like there was cold air blowing on my back, no matter what

I was doing. The cold air made me uncomfortable, and it was distracting. It made me feel exposed and anxious, like I had to keep pulling my shirt down in back to block the draft. I couldn't get away from it.

I started biting my nails and pulling my hair. Mom said, "You look like crap." Rhonda said, "Jeez. Let me introduce you to my brush."

So when summer arrived and I found out that, as a sixth grader, I had been invited to go to Hawthorne Youth Camp for a week, my first thought was that I'd be safe from Robbie for seven days. Because we were poor, Mom didn't have to pay, so she said yes.

She drove me to the place where we were all going to get on the bus. On the way she said, "I want to teach you something. On the ride your ears are going to start hurting. That's because you're going to be heading up the mountain where there is less oxygen." She explained that the change in oxygen caused a difference in air pressure and you felt it in your ears. I hadn't known my Mom knew things like that. She sounded almost like a science teacher.

I tried to hug her before getting out of the car, but she held me at a distance and said, "See you soon." I walked away from her, turning back once, to see her holding up her head with one hand and half waving with the other. She had a small smile in the corner of her mouth.

The camp was in a town called Wrightwood in the San Gabriel Mountains above Los Angeles. On the bus ride up I was stunned that so close to where we lived there was a completely different world, one with needled trees, like in Christmas stories, and giant gray birds that I'd never noticed before back home. The air stung my lungs. It felt sharper and fuller than down below where we lived. And Mom was right—my ears popped.

The road wound around and around, and we went higher and higher until we drove down a driveway that ended in a cluster of brown buildings. Just like at school, there was an American flag on a pole, but this one was waving in the breeze.

Every morning we would sing a song called "Rise and Shine" and then head off to cold showers in another cabin. We'd gather around the flag pole in a circle for the flag raising. Lunches were huge: chocolate milk, fruit cocktail, a square slice of pizza, corn, and a pretzel with mustard, all served on a blue tray with little pockets for each item.

Some kids I knew from school were there, but I avoided them and just hung out with new kids who wouldn't know anything about my family or me. I laughed loudest at their jokes, even the ones I didn't get, and flipped my hair the way one of the girls did when she was talking. I crossed my legs at the ankles when boys walked by, just like the other girls did.

Up there at Camp Hawthorne I became a different person, the one I believed was the real Risé. Everyone called me Rice, and said, "Rice is Nice," which made me turn red with pride and shame at the same time. At night, no one crawled into my bunk, which was mine alone. I slept soundly and woke up, alert and ready, to the "Rise and Shine" song belted out over the loudspeakers. One of my new friends said the song had my name in it, and she sang it to me.

The counselors were big kids, and they wore the latest styles. The boys and girls had long hair. The boys wore theirs like mops, the girls just straight down. In the pool and at Jackson Lake, the girls swam in plaid bikinis, and the boys in plaid trunks.

They warned us about black bears and rattlesnakes and mountain lions, dangers that never materialized. We rode horses. We walked trails. We made campfires and roasted marshmallows. We sang songs in the amphitheater, which was a half circle of rows of stone seats dug into the side of a hill. The song I remember the best is "The hot dogs at Camp Hawthorne, they say are mighty fine. But one jumped off the table, and bit a friend of mine. Oh I don't want no more of this camp life, gee Mom I want to go," but I would always change the words at that point to "I don't want to go" and I would belt it out at the top of my lungs.

TROPHIES & HOLY WATER

Grandma Foote went into the hospital for cirrhosis of the liver. She had always been one of my favorite people, and I had been hers. But when she was hospitalized, Mom told me I wasn't allowed to visit her. Then she died.

The night I found out I carved "I hate you" into the wall with the point of a dried out ballpoint. I wasn't sure who I was talking about exactly.

Soon after, I found out I had two other grandparents. We moved to a house six blocks away from Big Henry's parents, the Graczyks. They were pretty much the opposite of Grandma Foote. They were Catholics and liked their rituals. At Easter they had a priest bless their food before they ate it. Before eating anything even on regular days, they all bowed their heads and said, "Bless us, Oh Lord, and these thy gifts which we are about to receive from thy bounty, through Christ, Our Lord. Amen." Mom said, "I am a Catholic too, you know."

Grandma Graczyk kept a row of statues on the windowsill. She said they were Jesus, Mary, Joseph, St. Paul, and St. Frances of Assisi, who was surrounded by ceramic sheep. She told us whenever we got in a car to pray to St. Christopher who was the patron saint of travelers. When we wanted to wake up at a certain time, she said, we should pray to St. Benedict and tell him. When a dog pooped in her yard, Grandma Graczyk prayed to Saint Roch to keep it away.

I liked the idea that there was a saint for everything and a system in which you could ask for what you wanted and the outcome was all but guaranteed. I wondered if there was a patron saint to protect you against brothers, and I wanted to ask Grandma Graczyk, but I didn't know how.

I decided the food blessing made the food taste better, and even at home I would mutter the words before eating, although I jumbled them up and forgot some. Of course I made sure none of my siblings could hear me.

When Renee fell and scraped her knee, Grandma Graczyk dribbled what she called "holy water" onto the injury from a glass bottle and asked the Lord to send his angels to heal the wound. I thought it was probably just water out of the tap, so one time when I sliced my thumb open on a can, I ran it under the faucet and said, "Oh, Lord, bless this water and make it holy. And fix my thumb."

That same year a friend from seventh grade, Erica, invited me to a sleepover. I wondered if her home was going to be anything like the Graczyks' with the quiet prayers, and I wondered if I needed to practice.

But my worries were unnecessary. When I got to Erica's house, her mother opened the door and stuck out her hand to meet me. She had us sit down at the table in the kitchen and eat ginger snaps, which we dipped in glasses of milk. There wasn't a thing on the kitchen counters. At first I thought they just didn't own anything to leave out, but when Erica's mother opened the kitchen cabinets I could see that all their stuff was just put away.

Crumbs flew out of our mouths when we talked, and Erica's mother quickly scooped them up with a sponge.

Erica had her own bedroom upstairs with a white-framed bed. She had a red and white flowery bedspread and gauzy see-through curtains. She had put up posters of Simon and Garfunkel and Gary Puckett and the Union Gap on her walls. Her dresser was lined with silver cups. "What are these?" I asked.

"Trophies. This one's for track—the 50 meters. This one's for golf. I won a tournament last year. This one is for basketball, and this is volleyball, golf again, basketball, basketball, the 100 meters, basketball, and golf."

"You won all these?"

"Yeah," she said. "Want to do the Ouija board?"

I didn't know what that was, but Erica showed me how to ask it questions, like "Who am I going to marry?" We rested our hands on a little tray and it vibrated over to the number zero three times.

"That's weird," she said. We tried it for her, and it spelled out the name T-O-M, which made us laugh because there was a Tom in our class, but he was a dork.

I snuck a look at Erica when she was laughing. Her teeth flashed white like her polished bathroom toilet. Her hair was clean and frizz-free. I wondered how I could get myself a trophy.

In the morning, her dad made us pancakes and bacon. No one prayed, so I didn't either. I forced myself to chew the food slowly, like Erica did, and I only reached for more bacon when her dad asked me if I wanted more.

ENLIGHTENMENT

Robbie kept visiting me every few nights. It didn't matter how much I prayed, it didn't stop. It didn't matter how much I pretended to sleep, I couldn't. He would suddenly show up and rub up against me and touch me and hiss into my ear, pleading and pleading.

Our house had an alcove right outside Mom's and Big Henry's bedroom, like a little entryway. I decided to move a mattress into the space to be closer to them at night. I hung a sheet from the ceiling with tacks to give the space some privacy, and I brought my clothes there in boxes. I would always grab Big Henry's pillow from his bed and hold onto it before going to sleep. When he came home, late, from the bar or wherever he'd been, I was always awake, and he'd often stop and chat with me as he picked up his pillow.

One night he plopped down on my mattress. He stank of cigarettes. "Hey, Ruhruhruhrisay," he joked. "Shit, it's late. So why you sleeping here now? Is this for good?"

I shrugged.

He grabbed his pillow and hugged it.

"Big Henry?"

"Yup."

"You were raised a Catholic."

"Yeah."

"Which makes you kind of an expert on God stuff."

"I guess."

"So does Jesus actually listen to prayers and answer or is it more like you leave a message with his secretary?"

He had a good laugh. Then he said, "The way it was taught to me is you can communicate directly with Jesus, God, and/or the Holy Spirit. No secretaries. However, priests, who are kind of like God's office workers, will deliver messages too, and they kind of like acting like you've got to go through them first."

"So if I've been praying and I'm not getting an answer does that mean that Jesus just doesn't care about me?"

"Oh," he let out a laugh again. I get it now. You're

talking about the non-answering God. We've all been through that before. Let's see. What they always told us about that was that Jesus knows what's best for us, so even if we think we want something, we might be wrong about it. So, in a way, Jesus is actually doing us a favor by not answering. I think."

I was working through my disappointment over his answer when Big Henry said, "What did you ask for?"

"Nothing." But I gave him a pointed look.

"Look, honey, I'm pretty wasted right now, but my instincts are telling me it's not nothing."

I just looked at him again.

"What?"

He rubbed his head. His eyes were red like wounds. He gestured at my bed and the curtain and my boxes of clothes. "Does all this have something to do with it?"

I nodded.

"Hmm."

He turned his head toward me. "Your sisters bothering you?"

"No," I said. Then I decided to say one thing more: "Not them."

Now he looked right at me with his blood-red eyes. "Who?"

His reaction alarmed me. So I just shrugged again.

"Hey," he said, elbowing me. "Hey."

"It's just . . ." was all I could get out.

"Just what? Just who?"

"Robbie," I finally said.

Big Henry tilted his head to the side like he was getting seasick or something. He rubbed at his face and opened his mouth to crack his jaw. "Okay, okay," he finally said. "Don't worry about it anymore. I'll take care of it." Then he patted me on my head, stood up with his pillow, and went into the bedroom and closed the door.

That was it. No one said anything more to me about it, but Robbie never came back to my bed. The next day, Big Henry moved all three boys and their beds and stuff out to the garage.

I had been praying for almost two years and it turned out that all I had needed to do was say something to Big Henry.

I decided that I needed a different God, since the Christian one of the Kims and the Graczyks was apparently defective. I figured out just which God on my way back from the store with a pack of cigarettes for Mom and some candy I had shoplifted. Walking down the sidewalk toward me was a bald guy wearing an orange robe and beating a drum. I stared. I had never seen anything like him before.

"Hey," I called out, and he stopped. "Why are you dressed that way?"

"I'm a Buddhist."

"What does that mean?"

"You're divine. I'm divine." He held out his drum. "We're all vibrating to the beat of the cosmos."

I'm sure I looked confused because he kept talking. "It's about peace and light and freedom, man."

"Is there a God?"

"We're all part of God. Everything. The ants, the air, the trees."

I got up the nerve to ask my main question. "What if you don't like the way things are? Does God help you?"

The Buddhist patted my shoulder and looked into my eyes. "Pray to the universe. If you pray enough for anything it will happen."

Then he said, "Peace, man," and drummed away.

I checked out some books on Buddhism from the library. I liked that, like Catholicism, it came with accessories. From what I could gather from the books, I needed incense, beads, and maybe some little bells. I set up an altar in my alcove, using an old wooden crate and covering it with a green towel. Rochelle had some incense and I jammed a stick of it into an empty pop bottle. I pried the bicycle bell off one of the old bikes in the garage. I made a string of beads out of thread and coffee beans.

The rest was candles and scarves and rocks. I managed to shoplift a scarf that looked sort of Indian from a local hardware store. I draped that over the altar and arranged the candles and rocks and bell on top. I found an old carved wooden box on a shelf in the garage, and that looked good on the altar, and inside the box I stored a Canadian coin that Ted, the jerky clerk at the liquor store, had given me once instead of a dime. I made the joke to myself that it represented personal "change."

Then all I had to do was ring the bell, sit with my legs crossed in front of the altar, and, while counting on the beads, chant Nam-myoho-renge-kyo, which I decided meant, "Get me the fuck out of here." I understood that my goal in this practice was to get to a place where I didn't feel anything, and that sounded reasonable. Pretty soon I incorporated alcohol into the ritual too. I poured rum into a teacup and chugged it before my chanting. I read that I needed to tap into the connections among all people across all time. So as I chanted, I made my eyes go blurry and felt my spirit reaching out. Mostly, I reached for different people, people I hadn't yet met, and the future where I hadn't yet been. I told myself that no matter what had happened to me so far in this life, there was a better place and I deserved to be there.

After a week of chanting I found I could focus faster. My hands settled down, like tired butterflies perching briefly on a branch. I noticed things I hadn't before. I looked at my mother and decided I didn't need to be afraid of her anymore. I looked Robbie in the eye, and he turned away first. I saw that my sister Rochelle was putting on weight, fast, and Rhonda had terrible black circles under her eyes. Mostly I felt noticed, by the unseen universe, and it gave me hope that I could belong somewhere else. I elbowed Henry in the shoulder when I caught him trying to steal my box and coin. "Stay away, freak," I hissed. No one was going to mess me up now.

Two weeks later Mom told me I was going to go live with my Dad again. I guessed the chant had worked.

13

Thirteen was my age, in America it was a symbol of bad luck, and for Tibetan Buddhists it was holy. Some famous king, they believed, had been born with 13 flowers in his hands. He immediately walked 13 steps and swore he'd be a Buddha at age 13. There was something more too, like he had 13 concubines, 13 protectors, 13 mountains, I can't remember what else. Thirteen was the number of weeks Rochelle had been pregnant when she finally told us. And its opposite, 31, was the day in October I went to live with my father.

After Mom dropped me off, Bonnie opened the door, frowned, and said my Dad was at the bar working. Despite her crabby greeting I was hoping that this time living with them was going to be better than living at home where everything was chaotic and dirty. As I dragged my garbage bag of clothes and Buddhism gear into the house, I noticed that Bonnie looked a lot like my mother. Not as pretty or classy, but she had the same dark hair, similar dark eyes, and the same kind of light skin. The same little mean corner of her mouth. I realized that Bonnie and Mom didn't look much like me at all with my light hair, sharp nose, and square jaw.

She pointed at the girls' room and I dragged my stuff in there. Connie and Terry were sitting on their beds, apparently waiting for my arrival. They glared at me.

"Hey," I said. Connie said, "Hi," like it hurt her. Terry said, "I remember you." Connie shook her head at her sister, like they weren't supposed to be talking with me.

"I want to set up my altar."

Terry said, "What's a altar?"

Connie said, "It's for praying."

I jumped at the chance to be superior. "Not really. More like for chanting and meditating actually."

Connie made a face. Terry watched while I set up my crate with its scarf and candles.

Terry said, "Mama said no candles. 'Cause of fire."

Something was wrong with that kid. She was too old to talk like that. I looked at Connie, and she mouthed angrily, "She's retarded." That explained it.

"Well, Terry," I said, slowly. "I can light candles because I'm a teenager. Bonnie means *you* can't use candles. Probably not Connie either."

Connie said, "Dad can't use candles either. Mom said because when he's drunk he could start a fire."

"He's not your Dad. He's mine. And besides, she gets drunk too."

Connie frowned and crossed her arms. Terry rang the bicycle bell.

When Dad came home eventually, he gave me a hug and said, "Got some boobies finally." Although that was a weird thing to say, it seemed normal coming from my father. I was glad to see him. I had forgotten how energetic he was, not like the rest of my family, all sitting around and getting high or drunk. When Dad walked in, it was like he unsettled the dust and made things happen.

Bonnie served a dinner of Chef Boyardee and peas, I think because she knew how I felt about them. Dad smiled at me in between gulps of beer and said, "You're a good-looking kid. Taking after me."

That made me happy. Dad was noticing something special about me. And I liked the idea that we were alike. Maybe that's why I was so miserable at home:

I really belonged with Dad. And maybe that's why he had run away—he couldn't stand to be around the rest of them either.

After dinner Bonnie put a mattress down on the floor of the girls' room for me. I stretched a couple of sheets out on it and climbed in. I noticed that the girls were acting weirder than usual. Terry wailed, and Connie said, "It's ok. It's ok."

I wondered if they hated me being in their room or what.

I found out what a few hours later.

I was still having trouble sleeping even that far away from Robbie and so I was awake when the door opened and my Dad's large frame blocked the light coming from the hall, leaving him in shadow. I smelled his cologne. I wondered if he had forgotten to tell me something, but I watched him move toward Terry's bed. When he walked in and away from the doorway I could see he had on a red robe.

I was stunned for a while, unsure what was happening. I was jealous at first that he had come in to see Terry and not me. But then I heard rustling and some whimpering from Terry and then a vigorous repetitive sound that reminded me of Robbie. Then Dad went to Connie's bed and the same thing happened.

I tried to hold my breath. Tears exploded from my eyes like animals let out of a cage. They ran down my face, and into my mouth, salty and hot. My Dad finally left Connie and came to me, kneeling on the floor, just as I knew he would. He tried to pry open my legs. I used every muscle I had to keep them clenched together, but he won, easily. He wrenched me open. There was no pleading from him. I spent the rest of the night wide awake and shivering, sore, feeling sick.

The next morning, I crept into the kitchen, and he was already standing there in khaki pants and a plaid shirt. His hair was wet from his shower. He had his gold chain around his neck and his dress watch on his wrist, his sleeves rolled up exactly the same length on each arm. He said, "Morning, sunshine. I really want you living here. I'm buying you a bicycle so you can get to school."

I ran out of the house and threw up on the curb. I didn't go back.

MEMORY

My memories are tricky things. They come and go as they please. I can try to block them, but they usually take over so I don't even know I'm having a memory before it's too late. Other memories I try to corral, but they slip away and I can't retrieve them, like sneaky rodents. Like when I left Dad's house and ran back to ours, and my Mom wouldn't let me stay, even when I told her what had happened. Where did I go? I dig and dig through my brain, but I can't find it. Probably I stayed with friends.

One night that I do remember I spent at my best friend Kathy's house. We had been drinking 7 and 7s and I must have passed out on her couch. When I woke up Kathy was gone, probably in her room, and her Dad, an enormously fat man, was massaging my breasts, hard like he was making hamburgers. I told him to get off me, but he pinned me down with his huge weight and rammed his sweaty hand down my pants. He only stopped when I threw up all over the couch.

"Fucking hell," he shouted and lumbered to his feet. I didn't stick around to say goodbye to Kathy and ran out into the dark street. I wondered later if Kathy had left me out there on the couch like bait, and if I had saved her that night. My breasts, which had just grown big enough to jiggle when I walked, hurt, and I wrapped my arms around myself to hold them.

I remember another time I was standing in the middle of a parking lot. I don't remember how I got there now, but there I was, it was evening, and I looked up at the sky and noticed that it was orange. One star was already out, twinkling feebly. One huge parking lot with a bunch of empty cars, me, and that one star.

At some point during those months when I was homeless I chucked Buddhism. It was too hard to set up my altar every place I stayed, and praying hadn't changed anything. I tossed my wooden box, the incense, the bell, the scarf, and the beads into a trash can.

I can't remember now what was going through my head then but today if I try to think about thirteen-year-old me with no place to go I feel a pain under my heart, like someone's reaching in with a fist. The pain quickly becomes a white hot fury that blots out the image of the young girl. I can't keep the girl still in my mind. I still can't hold her there long enough even to say kind words or to put an arm around her shoulder. It will be okay — I can't say it. The danger is that something will give way and never stop.

Eventually I was allowed back home. Rochelle was huge and due in two months and soon there'd be another crying baby, but for now I could handle it. Robbie didn't come near me and still wouldn't look at me. He was mostly gone anyway. Rhonda was locked up in Juvenile Hall where Mom had put her for being an "incorrigible child."

Buddhism hadn't save me from anything, but the focus I had developed from the chanting and meditating was valuable. For example, I noticed where Mom had hidden some extra alcohol. I noticed that Raymond was hardly ever home and wouldn't speak to us much when he was around. I noticed that Rochelle seemed different than she had before. She hardly laughed. I noticed that Mom was eyeing me.

SLEEPOVER

In 1970, everybody knew the world was changing. People gathered on the streets listening to music, "I'll Be There," "Raindrops Keep Falling on My Head," "O-o-h Child," "Lookin' Out My Back Door." People said, "Far Out" to each other and "Can You Dig It?" Everyone was smoking and talking and drumming and dancing. I felt things were going to get better, not because of God but because someone—a person, like me—had finally pulled the keys from the grenades. Hair wound down like vines to waists, and pants widened at the bottom like spreading roots. Hope grew inside me like a stubborn weed.

Frustration with all kinds of things—rigid social rules, social injustice, war, and poverty—bubbled over and leached out into the world. Angry mobs set cars on fire. Soldiers shot students at Kent State. Rochelle told me Mexicans were marching down the streets of Los Angeles, but I didn't see them. Students battled police in Michigan.

Humans were waking up. And I was finally sleeping through the night.

I went back to work, doing all kinds of odd jobs so I could make money to buy clothes. When I bought something I hid it in a cardboard box so that no one would take it.

At night, Rochelle would toss and turn in her bed, trying to get comfortable. I thought she was so big that the baby might just walk right out of her.

When I was drunk and the radio was blasting, I was happiest. I could just climb up on the sound and ride it, far away, like it was the public bus. Sometimes I would dance, by myself, on the sagging porch, and pretend I was living a different life. In my head I lived in a clean house with really quiet children, the ones I would have had with my businessman husband. The only sound was the music. No one was coming to the door. I had nice things, I wore nice clothes. Peace ran through me and settled in my belly. All I had to do was breathe it in, and the chaos and fear and meanness would fall away.

No one was going to push me around—not anymore. I decided I would claim my place in the house, so I invited Kathy, Erica, and Candie to a sleepover. Rochelle was gone at her boyfriend's house. Renee was at Big Henry's for the night.

I cleaned up our bedroom in preparation, getting rid of the dirty underwear and stuffing our other clothes into the closet, and I put clean sheets on the beds. I snuck in a lamp from the living room and put a red towel over it, which made the light kind of weird, not cool as I had hoped, and I taped some pictures to the wall that I had found in one of Mom's old movie magazines. There were pictures of Rock Hudson, Mia Farrow, Raquel Welch, and Robert Mitchum. The effect wasn't exactly what I had wanted. I couldn't find pictures of the Stones or the Beatles or Joan Baez. The actors seemed old fashioned and made the room look kind of like an auto repair shop or maybe a soldier's barracks, so I added a few candle stumps on plates I had found on the edge of Mom's bathtub.

When the girls got there, we immediately went into my room and shut the door. I didn't want anyone from my family interacting with them. I had put Cokes and a bag of Fritos under the bed for refreshments. Erica showed up a little late with more candles and a plan to have a séance.

She had us sit in a circle, surrounding the candles. We made another circle around us with Frito crumbs. Then

Erica made us hold hands. She said, "Oh spirits, hear us, hear us. We call forth the ghost of the most famous spirit there is."

It turned out to be Jimi Hendrix, who had just died. The way we found out it was Hendrix was that suddenly "Hey Joe" started wailing from the living room. Wide eyed, we held our breath. I dropped my friends' hands and charged through the bedroom door and down the hall. The living room was empty, and the music suddenly stopped.

I returned to the bedroom where my friends waited for me to explain.

"There was no one there," I said.

Kathy said, "The music stopped."

"I know. Just when I got there."

Erica said, "Oh my God. It was Jimi. For real."

Candie said, "Oh, man."

We all started screaming and squealing and jumping on the beds. We had made a connection with another world. This wasn't the only place. We wouldn't have to be stuck here forever.

But just then my mother, not Jimi, showed up in the doorway. "Jesus Christ," she said. "I'm trying to get laid. Pipe down."

That was the last time my friends' parents let them come over to my house.

LOCKDOWN

The fury was building up inside of me, and there was only so much room in my small body to contain it. One day when I came home and Mom said, "Where have you been?" I couldn't stop myself from smarting off.

"Nowhere," I said.

"Nowhere? Don't you disrespect me."

I really couldn't help it. "Fuck you," I blurted.

Mom fixed her shimmering eyes on me. She paused, plotting. Then she said, "You go to your room and take out your best stationery and bring it here."

"No fucking way," I said. She advanced on me.

"You will do it."

I did. I brought it to her, and she told me to write, "I'm sorry for disrespecting my Mother" one hundred times on my good stationery that I had bought with my own money.

Instead, I wrote, "Fuck you," large, just once.

Mom said, "Go get the belt."

But I ran out the door. I ran all the way to a friend's house. Jill let me in. "Hey," she said. "Hey," I said back. "I've got to get out of my house."

Jill pointed at a bag of speed on the living room coffee table. "Should we?"

I nodded. So we took the bag upstairs to her room.

We started throwing the pills in our mouths like they were gummy bears. I told Jill that I hated my mother, and she said, "Who doesn't hate their mother?"

I was surprised by the idea that other people might be unhappy in their families too.

"Well, we could bust out of here."

The higher we got, the better the idea sounded. So Jill ran downstairs to get a road atlas from the living room, and then we spent an hour closing our eyes and randomly pointing at the map of the United States. Abilene, Texas. Winston-Salem, North Carolina. Springfield, Missouri. Lakewood, Colorado. Each place was a complete mystery and represented the opportunity to start out fresh, to be different people with different stories.

Our game was interrupted by a loud banging on the

front door. We peeked out Jill's bedroom window.

It was the police. "Holy shit."

Jill said, "How did they know?"

I knew the answer to that. My mother.

While Jill stashed the nearly empty bag under her bed, her mother led the cops upstairs.

"Are you Rise Myers?" The officers pronounced my name as in highrise. That was kind of hilarious since I was—high Rise.

"Yeah," I said back, kind of giggling.

I was right. They were only there for me. In my stoned condition, I tried to figure out how my mother had known to send them to Jill's house. It hadn't occurred to me that Mom even knew who my friends were.

They asked me to turn around. They handcuffed me and walked me downstairs and outside to the patrol car.

"What did I do?"

"Watch your head."

They drove me to the police station where they took my shoes away and put me in a cell by myself. It was made out of concrete and it was cold. I tried not to sit on anything because I was sure the whole place was infested with some awful disease. I was sick that my bare feet had to touch the grimy floor. After about half an hour a cop asked me if I wanted to make a phone call. I chose to call my mother.

"Mom," I said. "They've got me in jail."

She wasn't at all surprised. "Yeah, well, that's because

you're insolent, a drug addict, and a thief."

I said, "I want to come home."

"I wouldn't let you sleep in my backyard," she said, and hung up the phone.

I didn't feel sorry for myself while I was in the cell. I mostly seethed with anger. I paced, back and forth, back and forth. After about an hour, a police officer came to see me. She told me they couldn't release me unless I had a place to go. I knew it wasn't a great option, but I said I could stay with my Dad. Anything to get out of the cold, disgusting cell. But the officer told me that the social worker said that wasn't possible because my mother had told her my Dad had molested me. So the only place left was Juvenile Hall, the alma mater of my brother and sister.

Juvenile Hall was a fancy word for prison. We slept on hard cots covered with thin mattresses. They made us wear ugly flowery dresses and blue Keds. We had inspections during which we had to stand in the hallway facing the wall while the guards looked through our stuff to make sure we didn't have any drugs or weapons. They made us do stupid art projects, like coloring in designs. We were forced to work, ironing and cleaning. They even made us go to classes, but I can't remember what they tried to teach us.

Everywhere we went, we marched in a line. Time to go outside? Line up and march. Time to come back in? Line up. Need to visit the bathroom? Get in line. All of the windows had bars. None of the furniture moved. Everything was bolted down and had a lock on it. The message was, "We don't trust you at all, and you might even try to steal this ugly metal table if we didn't bolt it to the floor."

I spent two weeks in there, immediately befriending the largest girl I could find so she would protect me. I told her her Afro was pretty. I complimented her nails. I laughed at her jokes, and she made sure nobody messed with me.

But despite Sharlene's friendship and protection, I hated every second of being there. It was ugly, and my being there meant I was no good, a loser, a person with no class or judgment who was turning out exactly the way my mother predicted.

We all had to meet with a counselor in a big circle every day. The counselor, who sat on a chair, told all of us sitting on the floor that we had to take responsibility for our actions. "There are always options," she said. "The key in life is to pick the right ones. You girls have a pattern of picking the wrong ones."

Maybe she was referring to my choice of parents. I thought I must have been drunk when I picked them. That made me laugh.

"Do you think this is funny, Rey-suh?"

"No ma'am. I was thinking about something else."

"Well, stay focused on the here and now. This is where you are."

I didn't really know how to do that anymore, focus on the here and now. I tried to recall my Buddhism skills. But even as I was thinking about what the counselor had just said, I started to drift off, wondering if Robbie had molested my sisters too. Wondering if Dad had ever touched any of them. Then I started wishing for some alcohol or some uppers, anything to get me out of this place.

At the end of two weeks, Mom and Lisa came to visit me. Mom's eyes were as sparkly as diamonds and just as sharp. Lisa, who was only eleven but already my size, was wearing my clothes, the ones I had bought with the money I had earned from working.

We had to meet with the counselor. We gathered in a little room consisting of one round table and four chairs. Lisa pressed down my jeans with her hands when she sat down, as if to emphasize them.

Mom told the counselor that I was filled with rage. It was true. I was.

Just then Lisa piped up with her smart little assy mouth. "I'm afraid of her," she whined.

Which was exactly what she should be: afraid. I said, "If I have to stay in here until I'm eighteen, I'm going to kill her."

Mom raised up her hands as if to say, "See? What can I do?"

The counselor intervened. "Rye-suh, you're angry, right? You admit that."

How had I managed to get the stupidest counselor in the universe? "Yes," I said fake sweetly. "I am angry that my sister stole my clothes."

"When you came here to Juvenile Hall, you lost some of your privileges. That's what happens when you can't fit in with society's mores," she said, using a word I had never heard before. "The next step will be to go to a residence program for a year."

I realized I had two options: Stay stuck in an even more miserable place or lie like there was no tomorrow and regain my freedom. So I locked down my feelings and said, "You are so right. I made bad choices, and now I need to make better ones."

The counselor smiled. My Mom eyed me warily. Lisa looked worried.

Now the counselor turned to Mom. "You can see we've been working on these issues in here. Do you think Rice-uh could get another chance?"

Mom rested her chin elegantly on her hand. "I guess we're willing to give it a try. It's been very difficult. Still, I accept the burden we parents have to bear. But," she said, turning to me, "you come back and you've lost your privileges. You own nothing, no clothes, no bed. All that stuff you have to earn back."

I knotted my fury into a little ball and stuffed it down

my throat. "I understand."

So they released me from Juvenile Hall. I rode in the backseat of the car on the way home, shooting arrows of hatred into the back of Lisa's head. Mom bragged the whole way about how much work Lisa was doing around the house and how funny it was that Big Henry's children had turned out better than her own.

I looked out the window at the sad winos clutching their paper bags, at the working mothers dragging groceries up the steps of their apartments, at the dogs on leashes being forced to crap on dusty patches of dirt.

This was not the right life for me. There had to have been a mistake. I didn't belong here. As soon as we got home, I swore I would take off again, this time for good.

SEX

By age fifteen, my best friends, Candie, Kathy, and Erica, had all had sex. I had been molested, but I knew enough to know that wasn't sex. My whole life I had been surrounded by people screwing each other within earshot and, often, within view. For example, when I was twelve, I had been sleeping in Mom's and Big Henry's bed with them. They were both drunk. Big Henry climbed on top of Mom and started pumping at her. I slid off the bed and watched.

So I knew what was involved and, judging from my family, I was probably genetically programmed to like it.

People who were in love had sex. In my fantasies, I would make the man I fell in love with happy by giving him great sex, whatever that meant, and I really didn't know. But in my mind I was always on top.

After returning from Juvenile Hall, I set out to catch up with my friends and understand sex better, using my customary approach of thorough research and acting the part. I chose as a target a guy named Ed who had graduated from my high school a few years earlier. He had dated Rhonda for a little while and liked to brag about "popping girls' cherries," so I figured he was qualified. Ed had enlisted in the Navy and was about to be sent off to Vietnam. I decided that having no strings attached was safest, so if I didn't like it there would be no expectation of me having to do it again.

My friends told me not to go ahead with my plan. They thought I was doing it for the wrong reason, but I didn't listen, and one night I made sure to stop by Ed's parents' house with a bottle of cheap vodka. His parents' motor home was semi-permanently stationed in their driveway, and I went in as we had planned and sat on the edge of the double bed at the back, waiting for him to leave the house and sneak into the motor home without his family seeing. He showed up five minutes later, and we started drinking, using some glasses from the motor home kitchen cabinets.

Ed was way taller than me. He was six foot four and when he hugged me after a few drinks, my head only came up to the middle of his chest. He was handsome enough and had a big Roman nose that still wasn't as big as his ego. After our awkward hug, he said, "Hey, I have a way with the Myers ladies, don't I? I'm about to bag my second." It wasn't romantic talk, but I wasn't there for romance.

He kissed me, and it was disgusting, like he was a golden retriever and I had peanut butter on my face. He said, "Don't worry, Risé, I got this. I know how to satisfy the ladies."

He guided me back to the bed and eased me down onto it. Then he pulled off his shirt and started tugging off his pants. He pawed at my shirt and bra, which I had to help him remove. Then he yanked down my jeans and panties like he was pulling down the tailgate on a station wagon.

He was already erect and huge and I wondered how in the hell that was going to fit inside me. It didn't, not easily. Ed climbed on top and, then, with no further introduction, rammed his dick into me. I felt like one of those paper bags that boys blow up and then explode with their fists. I could feel myself tearing. Ed said, "Oh yeah. Nice and tight. Sorry I'm so huge." He started riding me, and with every thrust a burning pain seared up my middle.

"Fuck," I said, "I need more booze."

"Oh, sure, baby. It hurts a little at first." He paused to hand me the bottle and squeeze my breasts. "This massaging should help too," he said, and I wondered if he was an idiot. After a few more drinks I submitted to more torture.

Ed finally finished, dribbling all over my thigh. I looked around and saw that I had bled all over everything. My bladder felt like it had been punched. I could hardly stand straight enough to get my clothes back on.

Ed said, "Hey do you know any laundry tricks for getting blood out of the sheets?"

Now I knew what I had been missing.

ALTERNATE REALITY

When she was seventeen, Rochelle had her baby, named Arlene. I tried to help her set things up in the room. We hung a mobile made out of clothes hangers, string, and balled up socks. I poked feathers into the socks to make them look like birds and drew marker eyes on them. We put a towel on the dresser so she could change Arlene's diapers on it.

The house was crowded again, with Rochelle, Robbie, Raymond, Renee, Big Henry, Henry, and Lisa, and now a new baby. After Arlene came, I tried to stay outside as much as possible. I didn't want to help care for another baby that wasn't mine. And Mom was trying to get me to do more work around the house since she couldn't make Rochelle do as much now. Since it was summer, I could find a way to stay outside almost all day. If I wasn't at one of my jobs, I'd either hang out at the park with a friend or we'd grab sodas and walk around sipping at them. Sometimes we'd throw a tennis ball at a wall near the school or watch boys play basketball.

After the baby came, Rochelle and her boyfriend broke up. She got really fat and spent most of her time lying on the couch, playing with Arlene.

Time crept by, like a raccoon sneaking around looking for trash. The fall rolled around again. I would stop in at school every once in a while to see my friends and fail a test. After getting a report card with three Fs, two Ds, and a C in P.E., I pretty much dropped out. So then I focused on making and saving money. I felt myself growing tough inside, like a callus. These people wouldn't stop me. I would get out. I would have the life I was supposed to have, with a husband and children and nice things. Feeling sorry for myself was a waste of time.

When Arlene turned one, Mom surprised Rochelle by bringing home a cake from work.

"Here you go," she said. "I remember what a pain in the ass it was to have a baby at a young age."

Another summer, I was fifteen and babysitting and washing people's windows for money. One day when I was killing some free time by throwing acorns into a can in our yard, I noticed a stranger walking by the house. He had curly blond hair and a long mustache. He was wearing a tight T-shirt and jeans. He was handsome, but the thing that made me notice him was the way he tilted his head to the side when he walked, like he was about to ask a question.

I followed him at a distance to a house a few doors down. That's when I started a week of spying on him from the bush at the corner of our yard. He surprised me one day by sneaking up behind me. "Hey. How come you're spying on me?"

I jumped and tried to pull myself together, tugging down on my tank top.

He held out his hand. "My name is David."

I shook it but forgot to say my own name, so he asked.

"Ree-suh," he repeated. "That's cool. Unusual." I blushed. He wouldn't let the spying thing go, so I finally had to stumble through some explanation about how I was just wondering who he was, because he was new, and how we all kind of kept an eye on things around there.

"Really? I find that hard to believe. This neighborhood is kind of neglected, I would say."

I smiled and squirmed.

"You know what I think? I think you were looking for

something. That's what people are usually doing when they're spying, right?"

Once my secret was out, I started spying on David openly, walking with him down the block when he was on his way to wherever he was going. I'd wait for him on his front porch until he came home or left for the day. I met his roommates, two guys who, like him, were back from the Vietnam War, and David's uncle who didn't have anywhere else to live.

David introduced me to all his favorite music. He had made himself a waterbed frame that had built-in speakers and drink holders. It was octagon shaped, and there were mirrors on the ceiling right above it. You had to climb up three steps to get on the bed, which was covered in red velvet. It was like a throne. In the afternoons, I would hang out with him and his dog on the bed, gently rolling with the waves of the mattress, listening to Neil Diamond and Roberta Flack, and getting stoned.

When David got high, he would start talking, about all kinds of things. One of his favorite topics was what he called "mysticism," and which I soon figured out had to do with how you saw reality. "It's like this, man," he would say, "what we're seeing all around us is actually the illusion. But like when you're tripping then what you're feeling and sensing is what is real."

He took a long drag on the joint. "So like there's this

dude named Aldous Huxley who wrote a book about how mushrooms and LSD and other psychedelic drugs expand the mind, you know? He calls it the 'mind at large.' It's what we oppress, you know, like we're leashing it, like a dog, and it's all because of social rules. We create this symbolic structure that determines how we think about reality, but it's not reality, dig it? Even our biology messes with us. The Central Nervous System on purpose shuts down most of what we're perceiving. So we're walking around so unaware of what's actually happening. It's crazy. But psychedelics can free us from all that, and we can expand ourselves again."

He talked and talked. I listened, soaking up everything, including the feeling that it mattered and especially the feeling that I mattered enough for him to speak to me about such big things.

He said, "There are hundreds, thousands, of other worlds out there, and we're so tuned out, man. We need to reconnect."

I wanted to listen to him talk all day to me. I wanted him to look at me with the excitement he would get on his face when he was talking about ideas.

One day he said, "How old are you anyway?" I lied and said sixteen. He said, "You know I'm twenty-five?" I didn't but I nodded just the same.

Another time David told me about some guy named Carlos Castañeda and shamanism and Toltecs and other things I had never heard of. He talked again about LSD and altered consciousness. What stuck from it all was that David was trying to find answers. I curled up against him and breathed in the smell of his shirt, kind of sweaty but clean. Like me, he was looking for something better.

David said, "Do you know what's fucked up?"

I shook my head.

"The power imbalance in the world. Things need to be made right again, man, but the only way they can be is through an altered human consciousness."

When I was away from him I tried altering my own consciousness. I said to Candie at the park one day that she was tuned out to reality.

She said, "Huh?"

Only David seemed to understand that the world was truly fucked up. How was it possible people could live in filth the way my family did? This Huxley guy would probably say my family needed to wake up to the reality of our own family and home.

David said, "It sucks, man, that we're all walking around with blinders on. We don't see how frigging huge the universe is and how we're all connected."

I said, "Or even see what's happening in our own houses."

He nodded and dragged on the joint and exhaled, while squinting, "Yeah, anywhere. The principles apply, man, universally. That's what's so beautiful about it. We all need to blow our minds open and take it in."

David gave me some of his books: John Powell's *Why Am I Afraid to Tell You Who I Am?*, *Be Here Now* by Ram Dass, Kahlil Gibran's *The Prophet*, and books by Carlos Castañeda. I would mostly skim the books, reading the first lines of chapters, searching for something that applied to me. My favorite part of *The Prophet* was a passage about how your children are not your children. Gibran said something about how the children come through the parents but they don't belong to the parents.

That made perfect sense to me since it explained how I was so different from my parents. I did not belong to them. I repeated that to myself many times and asked David to talk about it.

He said, "Hell, yeah, Risé. Your parents are like a tour bus. They gave you a ride here, you know. So you thank them for the ride and then you get off the bus and walk to wherever you need to go."

I tried reading the Castañeda book, but it was too weird. David told me that it was about how we're connected to different worlds, and I wondered if there was a way I might open a door to enter a different one. He said, "Sure thing, kiddo. It's called LSD."

"What about alcohol and pot?"

"That too." And he lit up a joint. Maybe drinking all the time was a way of tuning into reality, a reality that seemed better.

David made money by driving a tanker truck full of gas. But one day when he came home and saw me waiting on the porch he said, "Celebration time, Risé. I got myself a promotion." The promotion was a nine to five job in the office of the same company.

So that night we had a party. David cranked the Doors and the Stones and we and his roommates and his uncle and a few more of David's friends who showed up danced and got high late into the night. I started dancing and hollering at the top of my lungs, "I can't get no satisfaction." And David sang back, "Hey hey hey, that's what I say."

About a week later, after we had shared about three joints and a bottle and a half of vodka, I finally got up the courage to seduce David. This is what people did, I knew, when they belonged to each other, and I wanted David to belong to me. I stretched out across his chest and started playing with the curly hair on it.

He looked at me, surprised for a second, and then rolled me onto my back. I pulled off my pants and he pulled off his, first setting down the joint on the headboard ashtray. Roberta Flack was singing, "The first time ever I saw your face," and I thought I was in love.

With no further ceremony, David began pumping into me, slowly, with his eyes closed, until he came, which didn't take too long. Then he kissed me on my forehead, took another puff from the joint, rolled over, and fell asleep.

FIVE STAR HOTEL

I kept hanging out with David. Sometimes we would have sex, and sometimes we wouldn't. Always, he would talk and we would get drunk and high. We often fell asleep side by side in his bed. I didn't care if we didn't have sex, but I worried that sex was a gauge of his interest in me. If we didn't have sex it might mean he wasn't interested in me as a person.

One time, I passed out on his couch, never even making it to his room. I woke up to pain. I opened my eyes and David's uncle was on top of me, breathing into my hair, and grinding into me. I closed my eyes and pretended I was still unconscious. Maybe I was.

After David's uncle zipped himself up and shuffled off, I gathered up my clothes and threw them on. I slipped out of the house, afraid to see David. I didn't know if I would be ashamed of myself or angry with him. I didn't want to find out. Instead I ran home.

Rochelle was out with Arlene so I had our room to myself. I slammed the door and fell back against it. Damn damn damn damn, I thought. The words *hate* and *stupid* welled up in me, mixed with the taste of bile, directed partly against the entire world and partly against me. The difference wasn't even clear: Where did the rest of the world end and I begin? There was something so horribly wrong with me, so disgusting, so vile that this would keep happening to me again and again. I must be sending out some sort of repulsive signal to the world, asking to be punished. It didn't seem to matter whether I kept my mouth shut or asked for help, got angry or tried to be good. The fucking universe was out to get me. And yet it had to be my fault.

I sobbed into the stinking carpet, and I guess I fell asleep because suddenly it was two hours later, the light had changed in the room, my hair was in my mouth, and my cheek had the carpet pattern pressed into it.

I stood up and changed my clothes. Then I gathered up all the dirty clothes. I made my way with an armful of smelly shirts and underwear to the laundry room.

Mom showed up at the door. She dropped a basket full of laundry on the floor at her feet. She was wearing high-heeled pumps and a silky floral dress.

"Where the hell have you been?"

"David's," I said.

"He's just using you, you know. Why else do you think he would be hanging out with you?"

"Because he likes me."

Mom snorted. "You need to stop focusing so much on David and start helping out more around the house. This isn't a hotel."

It just came out of me. "Really? I thought it was. Five stars. I guess now that Rochelle has a baby and can't be your maid you need me to fill in."

There was a pause, as we each digested what I had just said. My heart was pounding in my chest.

Then, like a trigger had been pulled, Mom charged me with her hands up and fisted. I grabbed her hands in mine and held her at a distance using all my muscles. Finally, I was big enough and strong enough to win over her. She wasn't going to have the last word or the last punch. We locked eyes, mine shining with triumph and hers with spite.

And then she kicked me between the legs.

STONE COLD SOBER

A few months later, Mom surprised the hell out of me again when she appeared in the doorway of our bedroom. She propped her head on her hand and said, "I joined Alcoholics Anonymous. I guess I shouldn't tell you the people we know who are in there too. That would be a violation of an unspoken contract."

"You're not drinking?"

"Nope. And you might want to follow my example."

That was hilarious. For all of my fifteen years it seemed Mom had been holding a cocktail, and I couldn't imagine how different she might be without alcohol.

But I didn't get to ponder the thought very long because she followed up the first news with another bombshell. "I'm also leaving Big Henry. For good. I can't be around him and his drinking."

Mom wasn't one to lob a few grenades. She always went for the nuclear missile. So she had more news for me. "We have to move. Again. Without Big Henry's salary, we're all going to have to do with less."

"There's one more thing," she said, and I didn't know if I could handle any more. "I'm suing your father for child support. Just saw the lawyer today."

"Well then maybe we don't have to move," I offered, hoping.

"Are you kidding? It could take months to get the money from that bastard."

So Rochelle, Rhonda who was back from Juvenile Hall, Renee, and I clambered into the station wagon with Mom the next day to go visit an apartment she had found in Gardena. It was a disgusting old building in a terrible neighborhood. The landlord hadn't even bothered to finish cleaning the place, and there were piles of trash on the floors. The water ran out of the faucet rust colored. There was a large jagged crack in a bedroom window. One of the stove's burners didn't work.

The landlord took us out onto the back steps to show us the "view" overlooking the alley. Just then the Gardena

S.W.A.T. team, dressed in hard black uniforms like giant cockroaches, went jogging down the alley, their rifles at the ready.

Mom turned to the landlord and said, "We'll take it."

The older I got, the harder it was for me to bear the conditions of our life. It was like I could suddenly see how we came up short in every way compared to everyone else. Rhonda was having sex with a lot of different boys. They would bring her Reds and alcohol. Robbie kept getting arrested for stealing. I was a failure at school and even my formerly alcoholic mother thought I was drinking too much. We kept moving down, into worse and worse places.

When I looked ahead at my life, it was a tiny spark at the end of a long, dark tunnel.

When we got back home that evening, Rochelle threw some dinner together while I rubbed Mom's feet. Raymond, who was ten, came home late, after we had eaten, when we were all sitting in the living room. Mom said, "Where the hell have you been? Did you get a loaf of bread?"

He said, "Forgot" and walked to his room.

Mom hollered for him to come back, he ignored her. So she went marching down the hall, pushed open his door, and then started beating him down to the ground. Her fury exploded like a carbonated wine. She sat on him and beat him until she was tired enough that I could pull her off.

I had discovered the answer to my question about what Mom would be like without alcohol.

VEGAS

The day after Mom beat up Raymond, I went to Candie's house after school. I told her Mom was moving us into a rat-infested crappy apartment and that I couldn't take it anymore.

"I want to get out of town."

She said, "I'll go with you."

I told her I had saved $500 from my assortment of jobs. Her parents had given her a car. With those combined assets we could put some distance between us and home. We decided that our best bet was Vegas because we figured we'd be able to get waitressing work there and the journey wouldn't use up too much gas.

So a few days later instead of going to school, we jumped in Candie's Dodge Dart and rumbled out of town. On the ride, Candie and I shared a bottle of vodka I had shoplifted and peanut butter and jelly sandwiches she had made. We got all the way to Barstow, about a two-hour drive, when the Dart broke down.

A minister who happened to be driving by on the highway stopped to help. We told him we were heading to Vegas to find work and that we were basically broke. He arranged for a tow truck and put us up for the night at the local Salvation Army. He made sure we got food and a chance to browse through the clothes in the Salvation Army store.

Although he was nice to us I didn't hesitate to pocket a $5 bill that had been left out on the store counter.

The next day the car was ready. We had to invest about one-fifth of our money into the repair. I immediately fell into a deep sleep against the window while Candie drove, as miles of desert stretched along the highway.

When we pulled into town a couple of hours later, the sky was overcast. The gloomy, muggy weather deflated our mood. Billboards for personal injury lawyers and bail bonds cast giant rectangular faint shadows across the pavement. Fast food restaurants looked just like the fast food restaurants back home. Everything was dusty and either brown or gray.

We eventually found our way to The Strip where the fancy hotels and casinos were. But it was only 10:30 in the morning, and there was hardly anything going on. The few people on the sidewalks looked like they were on their way to work, carrying lunch bags or briefcases. A few cabs and buses lumbered alongside us. The thousands of light bulbs on the casino signs were turned off, now dull and transparent. Even the fountains were still.

We looked at each other. Candie said, "Well, we need to get a place to stay." So we drove away from the casino part of town where we guessed everything would be more expensive, toward the shorter buildings and sadder-looking streets. We passed tiny stucco homes and dirt yards fenced in by chain link, small businesses that had to be failing, restaurants and bars with empty parking lots. Pay day loan shops, storage units, bartending schools. Lonely palm trees cast only as much shadow as telephone poles.

But suddenly we saw an oasis of flowers amid the dusty city, what was an otherwise dingy motel called The Bromeliad, and Candie pulled into the parking lot.

The exterior walls needed painting, the parking lot needed repaving, and the blue metal bannister along the walkway was chipping, but flowers covered almost every inch of space, which helped hide how down and out things were there. We decided we weren't going to do any better than that place since the rooms were just $15 per night. Right next door to The Bromeliad was a diner that was open twenty-four hours so we could get food too.

We unloaded our stuff into the dark and dreary room, which had two double beds, a desk, and a night stand, and then headed back into town to look for work. We drove around for two hours scouting for Help Wanted signs. But we couldn't find anything, so we returned to the motel to watch TV.

We spent almost a week like that, looking for work in the morning, hanging out at the motel in the afternoon, watching TV at night. I was starting to freak out. We were plowing through our money without even trying. And it was weird spending all my time with Candie—I even missed my siblings.

One afternoon, we took a dip in the motel pool, which was essentially a square of water baking in the sun. A dead army of insects littered the surface and dead leaves had blown into the water from the hundreds of flower bushes. I didn't own a bathing suit, so I swam in shorts and my bra. Afterward, we drank lukewarm sodas on some cheap plastic lounge chairs that were torn and caught at our skin. I closed my eyes and prepared to fry.

Candie poked my arm.

"Whuh?"

"There are two guys, two o'clock, checking us out."

I did my best to see by merely squinting in their direction so they wouldn't see me looking.

"Hot," I said, trying to sound cool.

Candie said, "Yummy," equally stupidly, especially since the two guys were nothing special. They looked to be maybe slightly older than us, post-high school. They both had furry sideburns and farmer's tans. One of them had a little pot belly, and the other an ugly tattoo on his arm.

It didn't take long for one of the guys, the one with the tattoo, to saunter over and sit down on the edge of Candie's chair. I saw that the tattoo was a man with wings. "Ladies," he said.

We smiled.

"You two girls staying here?"

"Yes. How about you?"

"Room 21 in specific. Hey, listen, we've got some drinks and a little weed too, if you get my drift. If the two of you aren't busy later, stop by."

I looked at Candie and she shrugged, but she was smiling, so I said, "Yeah. Maybe."

"Cool. I'm Hank. That over there is Bruce."

We told him our names and he said his room number again and then made some weird gesture with his hand, like it was a gun and he was shooting at us, in a friendly way.

Candie giggled as soon as he was out of earshot.

I wasn't sure about the two guys, but I liked the sound of the alcohol and the pot.

So that evening after we had hamburgers in the diner, Candie and I dressed up a little, she in a sundress and me in a skirt and tank top, and we put on some makeup. Then we walked down the concrete walkway to Room 21. I was desperate for a drink. The stress of living in this new city with no clue how we were going to survive was getting to me.

Bruce opened the door. He was missing a tooth and smelled like he had taken a bath in a bowl of liquid leather. "Hey, hey," he said, and immediately gave each of us a cup of vodka.

We all sat down on the double beds. They told us they had been in town for a couple of days. They were entrepreneurs, Hank said, and hitting up a convention downtown to line up some sales. We told them we were in town looking for work.

I had several refills and before long I was numb. Bruce put some music on the clock radio and invited me to dance. I didn't know how to do anything except sort of hang on him while he moved. So he told me to stand on his shoes, and I did and then we sort of looked like we were dancing.

Hank lit up a joint and handed it to Candie. Then he opened a bottle of rum and poured it into our Styrofoam cups. I chugged mine and I immediately started feeling like there was no connection between my head and my feet. I must have swayed because Bruce said, "Easy there" and helped me down onto one of the two beds.

Candie said, "I have to go to the bathroom," and she disappeared from my view.

I don't know what happened after that but I woke up to a dull pain between my legs. I was naked, and Bruce was on top of me, thrusting into me. I did my usual trick of pretending I was still unconscious.

Hank was watching, kneeling by the side of the bed and saying, "Ooh yeah, baby."

Candie was gone.

I closed my eyes again. Bruce pulled himself out of me and then Hank took a turn. I felt like puking but kept it down. When Hank was done, he and Bruce, both completely naked, leaned back against the headboard of the other bed and smoked a joint. I faked coming to, got up off the bed, put on my clothes, fast, and left. Hank and Bruce watched me the whole time and said nothing.

Back in our room, Candie was sleeping. I shoved her. "Where the fuck were you?" I said, my voice reaching a panicked pitch.

She struggled to wake up. "Oh. My head."

"Why did you go?"

She touched her head and paused. "I was feeling sick, I think. What happened?"

"You left me and the scumbags raped me."

She grabbed the sides of her head. "Oh shit." She added, "Both?"

I started to cry. I didn't want to, but I was in some kind of endless loop. No matter what I did to change things, there was the same result. No matter whether I tried to be kind or to work hard or to pray to this God or to meditate under the eye of that one, no matter who I trusted or didn't, no matter anything, I ended up in the same place: on the trash end of everyone's leftovers.

Candie swore some more and said, "I'm sorry," twice. Then she started crying and called her parents.

I spent the day curled up on the bed, facing away from Candie who stared stupidly at the TV, mindlessly changing channels. Later that afternoon, her parents showed up in the motel parking lot in their motor home. Candie and I shuffled out of our room with our stuff. Her mom covered her mouth and shook her head when she saw me. She touched the back of Candie's head. Her dad wouldn't look at me, but he carried my garbage bags of clothes up the steps of the RV.

On the long ride back, Candie sat in a swivel chair up in the front, near her parents. I mostly slept, stretched out on the motor home couch. But every time I woke up,

I started crying. I didn't even know why. I had no right to feel sorry for myself since I had willingly gone into a hotel room with two jerks. I was furious with Candie for abandoning me, but I was even madder at me.

When we got to Candie's house, she and her mom went inside. I carried my bag down the steps of the RV. Her dad waited for me on the sidewalk. He handed me a wad of cash.

"Look," he said, "This is to help you get started."

"Thank you." I reached toward the money.

"There's more for you where that came from."

I started to pull my hand back from the green bills. He added, "All you have to do is meet with me once a week. Like for an hour. That's all."

GENIUS

Weeping, I walked fast down the sidewalk away from Candie's dad. A few blocks later at a gas station, I used the few coins in my pocket to make a call to Big Henry. I asked him if I could live with him, and he said yes. He drove to pick me up.

Big Henry had his own bedroom and had fixed up rooms for Henry and Lisa. I would sleep on the couch, the one he and I sat down on so we could talk.

"Vegas?" he said.

I was embarrassed. The way Big Henry said it, it felt

cheap and stupid.

"Why did you guys decide to come back after only a week?"

I didn't want to tell him what had happened. So I said, "It didn't work out there." I added, "I just can't be with Mom."

He nodded. "I know the feeling."

"She said *she* kicked *you* out."

He laughed. "That's not how I remember it. We weren't even talking to each other this whole last year. Did you notice?"

I hadn't noticed. Then he said, "You've never been in love. But once you have, you'll find out what it's like to fall out of love too."

That made me sad. Not for Mom, but for me, because it felt like he had fallen out of love with us, with me.

I could not understand why no one cared about me. After everyone went off to their rooms for the night, I broke down into heaving sobs, moaning and gasping for air. Why was I even born if it was just to feel again and again that I shouldn't have been? David would say none of this mattered, that it was just a learning journey anyway. I remembered a line from *The Prophet* about joy and sorrow, something about how they're a pair and when one is sitting with you at the table, the other is sleeping on your bed.

I pressed my face into the fabric of the couch and wept until my body couldn't push out another tear.

I settled into life on Big Henry's couch. Lisa avoided me—I think she was frightened I might follow through on my promise to kill her. To pay my share of the rent, I sold pot to my friends. Big Henry would give me a pound of pot and I would break it up and sell 1-ounce packages for $10 and then give him the money.

I would visit David too and stay at his house sometimes, but I always made sure his uncle was out before I went over there. One time there was a girl with David. Neither of them seemed to care that I was there too so I hung out with them, getting stoned.

I got some other side jobs, mostly waitressing. Since I was hardly going to school, I had a lot of time to work. Pretty soon I had saved up enough money to get my own studio apartment. It was pre-furnished, so I didn't have to worry about buying much when I moved in. The rent was good because the neighborhood was full of drug addicts and prostitutes. I kept everything spotless.

One day after I moved, I decided to visit Mom and Rochelle and Raymond and Renee at their apartment—Robbie was living on his own somewhere. It looked a little better than it had that first time I'd seen it—the trash had been picked up, for example, and now there was furniture. There were also dozens of Post-Its everywhere, which wasn't exactly trashy but it was strange. I guessed it was an AA thing. Mom had a note on the fridge that said, "Believe in yourself." There was a note on the bathroom mirror that said, "You are all you need." There was a note on a bedroom door that said, "Raymond, clean your room."

Everyone was out but Mom.

She said, "Do you want a drink?" I don't think she had ever offered me a drink in my life.

I failed to control my facial expression in time. She said, "I don't have alcohol, of course, but obviously that's what you were thinking." Instead she served me a glass of cloudy water from the tap, even though I didn't answer.

We sat down at the kitchen table.

She said, "Rochelle is fatter than ever."

"Where's Arlene?"

"There's a lady in the neighborhood does some day care."

"You hear from Robbie?"

"Are you kidding?"

My Mom fixed her eyes on me. "So you and Big Henry best friends now?"

I told her I had my own apartment. She said, "You think it's a good idea to live alone?" I said nothing.

"Well, I have news too," she said. "I'm in college. El Camino Community."

She looked at me carefully to see what my reaction would be.

I didn't know how to react, so I asked, "You like it?"

"Of course. It's what I should have been doing all along. You know they gave me an IQ test when I enrolled."

"Oh yeah?" Again, I didn't know what to say.

"I got a 160. That's genius level."

Mom was always leveling me with her news. It was strange enough that none of her kids were going to college but she was. But the genius part was truly shocking. I knew she was clever, but I didn't think she had brain power like that. Obviously the genes had skipped me altogether.

Like she was reading my mind, she said, "You could probably manage to finish high school at least."

The sun started setting as I sat there with my mother in her dismal kitchen that would never be my kitchen. As the light in the alleyway gradually faded and we talked about my siblings, the court case she'd won against my father, Big Henry, and AA, I felt everything from the past few years rushing at me.

I have no idea what season it was then, something that rarely mattered to me anyway in seasonless L.A. Whether it was May or November, the sun still set every night. It would rise again in the morning over the vast, flat city, over the heads of the millions of people who were getting ready for school or work, who were crying alone in their rooms, getting hit, or taking hits off bongs or from bottles. I thought about all the kids in L.A. schools who were getting Fs from teachers who didn't give a shit about them, all the kids getting raped by strangers or their own family members, kids and old people going to churches and temples, reaching out to a God who didn't answer, everyone desperate for love and willing to do just about anything to get it.

From the moment I first clawed at my polio-stricken mother's feet, begging for her attention, I had wanted something else, something more. And against reason, I had always believed I would get it.

Mom took a swig of the cloudy water and, looking at the bare wall behind me, said, "Your father impregnated me when I was fifteen. I sacrificed my youth and made sure you were all raised. Now it's my turn. At last."

I wondered if it would ever be mine.

Part II
Hear The Angel Voices

GRAVITY

My whole life I have felt the tug from some other aspect of life—call it another dimension or another spiritual plane. I've always felt the pull of forces larger than me. I've spent half my time looking for a way in, a way to connect—and the rest running away.

Again and again, the gravity of the universe has worked to tug me into my own body, my own experience. I've felt the strength of a horde of angels trying to wrestle me down, to be here, present, back from the brink. Feel it, they shout. Live it!

But I've also been pinned down too many times on this earthly plane by selfish humans, so my first instinct has always been to close up and run. Shut down the spiritual airwaves buzzing in my brain, so I can be at peace. A drink or a pill or a joint, anything to set me free for just a little while to get rid of the feeling of being pulled, of falling back into my life.

I have begged and pleaded for a way out. Please, I've prayed, please don't make me be here in this body, in this family, in this pain. Please take me away, help me escape. Please, please, please.

But what a mistake and a waste of time all that begging was.

As it has turned out, I didn't need to keep asking and begging and pleading for what I wanted, which didn't seem to do any good anyway. All I needed to do was learn to listen. The voices were there, asking me to hear what they had to say.

FAKING IT

I didn't graduate from high school. I never went to college, but the job market kept wanting a degree, so along the way I faked it. Just like when I had been a little girl, if dropped into an unfamiliar environment, I would play along as if I had inherited the role.

So when I left home for good at fifteen after the Juvenile Hall experience, I pretended to have a high school degree and a higher age for a job at Bob's Big Boy. It was easy. When I filled out the application, I wrote 18 next to Age and I made a little check mark in the box next to

High School Graduate. Even when I was selling drugs for Big Henry, I would lie about my qualifications, telling customers I was paying my way through college or saving up to "study abroad."

David was going to dental school at night. So I went to night school too—for me it was reading David's books in his room when he was gone. I read Ram Dass talking about caterpillars becoming butterflies. He said something about how you can't be a butterfly as long as you're busy being a caterpillar. You have to finish with one stage before taking up the next.

I tried to let go of my desire to be a butterfly so that I could in fact hurry up and be a butterfly. Alone in David's room, I read Powell, who said that the only way to achieve maturity was through communication and interaction, and I made a mental note to interact more. I read Gibran who wrote about working with love, which was a way of becoming more connected to yourself and to God.

So I threw myself into work with a fierce determination that I called love.

At my fast food jobs, I learned to make eye contact with people asking for more ketchup packets and the sad man who every day bought himself three double burgers for his lunch. I made sure to give my customers what they needed so I could get what I needed, which was approval, advancement, and money. When I stole from the register,

I did it better than I had before so I didn't get caught.

This was my plan: Watch people, especially the successful ones, and do what they do, just like them, and then make it better.

Living away from my family helped. The behaviors I was trying to copy seemed more normal among other people so it made copying them easier. I still felt like an actor, but now I lived on the stage.

Sometimes my fast food customers would ask me questions about my personal life. I would lie to make myself more interesting. No, my parents are dead. I have one sister. She lives in New York City. I'm going to night school. My father was an actor. My mother was a teacher. I'm studying accounting. I'm studying to be a paralegal. My dream is to start my own business.

When I turned seventeen, faking it got me a waitressing job at a diner. I told the manager I was twenty-one and had previously worked at a small casino in Las Vegas. Unfortunately, I told him, the casino had closed so I wouldn't be able to get him a reference. But I had been employee of the month there, twice. I handed him a résumé, filled with false information and on which I spelled the word *college* like this: collage. But I still got the job.

I had started living with David, and I told him about the job. He quoted Ram Dass at me: Something about expecting nothing and seeing everything as steps on a path. I wasn't sure what he meant, if anything, but it certainly deflated my news.

We spent every evening getting blasted. But in the morning I would force myself out of bed and into uniform, and I would make sure to show up at the diner on time. David wouldn't even notice when I got up.

At the diner, I copied the movements of the other employees, stashing my notepad in my apron pocket and my pen behind my ear. I made small talk, just the way the other waitresses did, and I learned to laugh at my customers' jokes. My goal with each table was to get them to love me so I could earn the biggest tip.

AL

One day, a Monday I remember, two older men sat down at my table. One had a thick head of wavy salt and pepper hair, thick dark eyebrows like the men in my family, and a kind face—so he seemed at once familiar and also entirely new. The other was balding and had a graying beard. I asked them if they were ready to order, and the thick-eyebrowed one said, "How do you feel about the fact that it's your job to take orders?"

I said, "I like my job."

"Yes, but you just asked if we were ready to order, and

I'm thinking how strange that is. We're going to give you an order, and you're going to take it."

His friend rolled his eyes and said, "Here we go."

I said, "I don't know. I hadn't thought about it."

The man came back on Wednesday and sat in one of my booths. For some reason, I was happy to see him. Before telling me what he wanted to eat, he said, "What are you going to be when you grow up?"

"Excuse me?"

"Well, is being a waitress your goal or are you thinking beyond this?"

I told him that I wanted to be successful.

"And for you what does that mean?"

I wasn't sure. But I thought about it all night and all the next day, and when the man came back on Friday with his friend and sat in my booth again, I told him, "It means I don't have to rely on someone else to be safe or happy."

The man held out his hand. "Baby, I'm Al. This handsome devil is Ken."

Ken said hello and gave me a big smile.

I asked Al if he was a psychiatrist. "Because you ask me so many questions."

He said, Let's have lunch, you and me, tomorrow."

I don't know why, but I trusted him, although, even as I was agreeing to lunch, a voice in the back of my head was warning me not to listen to my instincts because my instincts had up to that point in my life been defective. I ignored that voice and went to lunch anyway. We met at a fancy restaurant, where the choices on the menu had funny names like Frog Legs Meunière and Crawfish Croquettes. Al had to explain what they were and I chose the simpler-sounding Grilled Pork Chop.

Over lunch, Al told me funny stories about Ken, like about how Ken was afraid of the Ferris Wheel at the Santa Monica Pier. I pretended I knew what that was. He also asked me lots of questions, like about where I had grown up and what my favorite subjects were in school, to which I replied, "Zero." But he didn't do any of the things I expected like eye my breasts or try to get me drunk and then out into his car with him. I thought about Ram Dass again and wondered if he was right about not having expectations and just following the steps along the path.

Al and sometimes Ken started coming in for lunch five days a week, always sitting at my table.

Sometimes Al would tell me a joke, sometimes he would ask me a question and I knew it was serious and I had to come up with a good answer. Like he'd say, "If you could be anything what would it be?" Or he'd say, "Is it better to be happy or to be successful?" Ken would laugh and call him an asshole, but I would think about the question and then come back with their meals and an answer.

.

A NEW SMILE

Because of my drug use—including occasional coke—and complete lack of dental care growing up, my teeth had pretty much all rotted away by the time I was sixteen. I had never smiled by showing my teeth. Mom had taught all of us kids to smile with our mouths shut so that no one would see the gray, rotted mess inside.

But my decaying mouth was so distressing and shameful to me that I finally couldn't take it anymore. I had been on my own for two years, and I decided it was time to do something to take care of my problem. A co-worker recommended a dentist so I went to his office. I said, "Please pull out all my teeth."

A tall, skinny, good-looking man with a kind face, he said, smiling, "I don't pull teeth."

"But look," I said, opening my mouth wide.

He shook his head and poked at a few teeth with his finger. "Hmm. I can fix this."

"But," I said, "I'm just a waitress. I don't have that kind of money. Wouldn't it be cheaper just to yank them out?" The only thing I had to my name was an old car, and it was only worth about $125.

He made the *hmm* sound again and then massaged his jaw, like he was thinking deeply. "I'll tell you what," he said finally. "I'll work with you. We'll start at the front and work our way back. You have to promise me we'll do them all."

"But what about the money?"

"You'll pay, but slowly and over time, when you can."

I couldn't believe that a stranger cared enough to save my teeth. I threw my arms around him. "Okay, okay," he said, and gently set me back in the chair.

So I started my mouth rehabilitation. I would work all day and put money aside for gas or rent or whatever, and I would give the rest to the dentist. In exchange, he gave me root canals, gold posts, and crowns, and patiently waited for me to pay him back, slowly, like, well, pulling teeth.

I fell madly in love with him, the second kind man in my life. I would have done anything for him, but he kept things at the doctor-client level, offering kindness and professional service with the right kinds of strings attached.

A FRIEND

Al turned out to be a really good listener, so I started telling him everything, and I told him the truth. Like I told him about when Dad tried to drown Mom in the bathtub. Or when Mom had me arrested.

Over time, he came to know everything about me, including what we came to refer to as "the rapes and molestations," or, later, R&M in shorthand. When I first told him about Robbie, who we were now all calling Robert, he grabbed my hand, making me jump, and looked me in the eye and said, "I'm sorry, baby, that that happened to you." I couldn't help it—tears immediately gathered in the corners of my eyes and made everything blurry. I believed him. It was the first time anyone had ever said that to me, that they were sorry about what I had gone through.

We started having dinner together once a week, his treat, and then twice a week. Al took me to the Velvet Turtle, Millie Riera's Sea Food Grotto, The Admiral Risty, places with amber glassware, semicircular wooden chairs, soft piped-in music, and low lighting.

I found out Al and Ken ran a mold-making business, fabricating plastic or metal shapes that you would pour liquids into. It was a funny job that I never would have imagined.

Al surprised me by telling me he believed in past lives and spiritual healing. I asked him what he thought I was in a past life, and he said, "What do you think you were in a past life?" I said, "A wife and mother."

He said, "Yeah, probably. But that's not really much of a guess. Take a risk."

I said the first thing that popped into my head: "I was rich."

Al smiled. "That's more like it."

One of the most important things that came out of our conversations was that I found out what my family looked like to someone who didn't know them.

"It's a rotten shame what they did to you," he said simply.

I was intrigued by the idea that to the outside world my family's behavior might seem terrible. I wanted to hear more. "Well, I probably could have tried harder," I said.

One of Al's eyebrows went up. He said, "Tried harder?" I nodded.

"You were not the problem. They were." I wasn't sure I believed him back then, but I sure did love hearing it.

I also told him about David, and showed him a note he had written me on Christmas Eve. It went like this:

> Love one another, but make not a bond of Love.
> Let it rather be a moving Sea between the shores of your souls.
> Fill each others cup but drink not from one cup.
> Sing and dance together and be joyous, but let each one of you be alone.
> Give your hearts, but not into each other's keeping
> And stand together yet not too near together.

All Al said was, "Baby, you're not his girlfriend. It's time to get a place of your own."

If I had come up with the idea myself I probably wouldn't have followed through. But when Al said it, I knew it was the logical thing to do. So I let him help me find an apartment and move into it. And he helped me get a job at a better restaurant, Carrow's, which was part of a classy chain.

He then switched his weekly lunches to Carrow's, again at my table. Sometimes he would show up with Ken. We would talk every time I came by the table. He left me really good tips.

I found out Al had a number of girlfriends. They tended to be about twenty years younger than him and about ten years older than me. Like we were best buddies, he confided that he had a thing for breasts, so I started calling him Boob.

Part of me wondered why he didn't think of me the way he thought of his girlfriends, and part of me was relieved he never did. And part of me was mad at him for having girlfriends when I knew he was married.

Most of all, I couldn't understand why a man would want to have anything to do with me if it wasn't for sex. Regardless, it was a miracle to have a friend.

DOWNHILL SKIING

For my twenty-first birthday, Al and Ken took me and my friend Brenda to Las Vegas for the weekend. On the flight, TWA gave me a bottle of champagne to celebrate and a pin for my lapel. In Vegas, Brenda and I had our own room at the Sahara, and the four of us went to the MGM and saw Dean Martin. We all went dancing, and Al, it turned out, was a fantastic dancer.

It was a vastly different experience from my first time there. For a few days I felt like my life had completely transformed and that I was a completely different person than I had been days before at age twenty.

Over the next few months, I told Al more of my sad stories. Like I told him about how Mom had kicked me between the legs that one last fight we had. I told him how I had started writing my Mom bargaining notes because I was afraid to talk to her face to face. So, for example, I'd write, "Mom, if I scrub the toilets can I go with Candie to a movie?" Then there would be two check boxes, one marked Yes and one marked No. I'd even provide the pencil.

The more I talked to Al, the more angry I felt, like it was all happening to me again, only this time I was aware that I was mad about it. One time, over lunch, I slammed my hand down on the table during a story, which startled about ten people.

Al leaned over, "Let's keep it down so we don't kill anyone tonight, okay, baby?"

After that, Al came up with the idea that maybe I would benefit from therapy, so I found someone and started seeing her every week. She would ask me to talk, and I would start dumping all over her like I was a giant rain cloud and she had poked a hole into me. Then she would say, "How did that make you feel?" I would talk and talk, nonstop, and the therapist hardly ever got a word in edgewise.

All the talking was expensive, and Al pointed out that my Dad had caused some of the problems I was having so maybe he should pay for the therapy. That made sense, and one weekend I called my father.

He said, "Risé! Have you masturbated yet today?"

I ignored him. Rather woodenly I said, "Dad, I have been going through a really hard time because of lots of stuff that happened to me when I was growing up. You know about some of that stuff." I waited to see what he would say.

"You should come over and see me. We'll get Robert too and go get something to eat."

"I'm not coming to see you. I'm working and I'm in therapy."

"Therapy? You don't need that crap. You're perfect the way you are."

"Dad," I said, feeling myself losing control of the conversation, "I need therapy. It's helping me work through some stuff. But it's expensive."

"You're darn right it's expensive. Those fucking doctors charge what, like $50 an hour just to tell you blah blah, get over it. Why don't you pay me, and I'll do it?"

"I have a therapist already. I'm calling to see if you would pay for it or at least help me pay for it." As an afterthought, I said, "You did a lot of damage to me."

"I'm not getting involved in that shit," he said, and then he asked me if I wanted to come over for a barbecue.

In light of his answer, I took a break from counseling. I decided that maybe I just needed to reconnect with my siblings, that maybe we were all growing out of the misery we had grown up in, and that wallowing in it with a therapist was probably unhealthy anyway.

Since I was trying to reconnect with my family, and was inspired by Al's gift to me of the birthday visit to Vegas, I decided to take Raymond on a trip for his sixteenth birthday.

I planned for us to go downhill skiing. I had a brand new Toyota Celica, I had a little money now that I didn't need it for counseling, and I was proud. This trip would be an opportunity to give Raymond a view of what life could be like and to show him a good time. Our plan was to drive up to Mountain High Resort in Big Pines Park on Highway 2. Raymond came to stay at my apartment the night before so we could get an early start the next morning.

He looked around my apartment, not saying much, and then he asked if we could watch TV. I made him dinner, mac and cheese from scratch, and we watched *Valley Forge*, a movie about George Washington they were showing on TV. We curled up on the couch under a blanket as the Revolutionary soldiers were freezing to death.

At bedtime, I set Raymond up on the couch, giving him sheets and a pillow and the blanket. I went down the hall to my bedroom and fell asleep fast, almost vibrating with happiness over the gift I was going to give my little brother the next day.

I woke up with him in my bed, pulling at my clothes.

The first thing was to get away. I left, fast, and went to the living room and perched on the couch where Raymond was supposed to be. My hands were bouncing around so I lit up a cigarette. Little pictures flashed in my head: Robert, my Dad, other men. I was not in the pictures. I had disappeared.

I prayed, lamely, "What do I do, what do I do?" What would Al say? Al would tell Raymond to get the fuck out of my life.

And then I got mad. I sucked in the anger, like nicotine from the cigarette, and I held it in. I marched back into my bedroom. I did not turn on the lights. I said, calmly, without really knowing the first part to be true, "Sex is a great thing, Raymond. But not with your sister."

He didn't move. He was pretending to be asleep.

WRANGLING ANGER

Speaking with the therapist and my lunches with Al were starting to scratch at my emotional scabs. I was seeing more, understanding more about my family, and dealing with the greater self-awareness and increasing insights by drinking more often and taking more drugs. At work, I would pop speed in the walk-in cooler. Whenever things started spinning around in my head and I started feeling out of control, I would go "get a stick of butter" in the cooler and throw back another little white cross pill.

But one day I discovered I was not alone in the fridge. A co-worker named Sheila, who was probably about twenty years older than me, had just hauled in a carton of burger patties. I didn't hear her because she was toward the back of the cooler and bending over to lift the box. The door would swoosh loudly as it closed and it must have masked any noise she was making. Anyway, she stood up just as I was swallowing a couple of pills from a plastic bag.

"What are you doing?" she asked.

All I could come up with was "Nothing."

"Don't look like nothing."

"Why don't you fucking mind your own business?"

She didn't know how to butt out. "It *is* my business if a coworker is high and doing a crappy job."

Sheila's inconvenient presence and self-satisfied attitude made me go bat shit. It was as if every crummy thing that anyone had ever done to me suddenly manifested itself in Sheila, and she became the single biggest irritant in my entire life. I lunged at her and shoved her against the back wall.

She managed to get out a surprised "You bitch," which only fanned the flames. I grabbed onto her hair and started yanking it back with one hand while I clawed at her neck with the other. She succeeded with a few weak slaps, but I had the advantage of years of practice, the speed of youth, and the fury of the abused. I cuffed her across the face, hard, and then sent her reeling against the wall again. Her head made a loud cracking sound. "Jesus," she exclaimed, and I rammed my forearm into her neck. "Don't you ever," I said, "fucking get in my face again or I'll kill you."

I gave no thought to how I would get out of the mess I had just sunk myself into. Instead, I marched right on out of there and headed home, saying nothing to anyone.

The whole drive home, my brain felt glassy, like sloshing water, and I couldn't think clearly. It wasn't until I had been pacing for about half an hour that things started coming back into focus again.

"Holy shit," I said to myself.

Not only had I probably just lost my job but, far worse, I had probably given myself a fast pass to jail. Everything I had been striving for, all the effort to turn my life around and make things better for myself I might have just flushed away in one moment of blind rage.

I was too ashamed to call Al. All I could do was pace, throw down some beers, and try to get a handle on my internal turmoil.

I spent the whole night and the whole next day, my day off, freaking out, terrified that at any moment the police were going to show up.

But they didn't and when morning came around again, I got up and put on my uniform and drove to work. Sheila was there. She didn't look at me. She didn't say a word. But the restaurant manager came up to me and said, "What the hell happened to you the other day? You can't just leave without telling me. If you've got your lady issues cropping up and you need to go home you still have to tell me, got it?"

I nodded and mumbled, "Sorry." I couldn't believe my good luck. I decided right then I was done losing control over my anger. It was too risky for me.

CHOICES

David called and told me he was selling all his stuff, including his house. "I'm going on a road trip. Got to find some more answers."

"What about Mella?" That was his dog.

"She's coming with me."

I would miss his house, not that I went to see him very much anymore, and I would miss Mella. I was glad he wasn't leaving her with one of his roommates.

We agreed I would join him and Mella for part of the trip. I decided to spend a week with him in the Badlands.

So I drove east to Deadwood, South Dakota, to meet him. From there we convoyed to his campground and started a few days of hiking and cooking hot dogs in the fire pit.

One night we were curled up in sleeping bags in David's tent. Mella, who was stretched across our feet, was dreaming and her paws were twitching. I was leaning on my elbow looking at David and admiring his strong profile, one of his best features.

I hadn't seen him in a while and seeing him now reminded me of seeing him the first time when I started spying on him. And that made me think about how he and his roommates had just come back from Vietnam. That hadn't meant much to me at the time, but now I realized it was strange that we had never, in all our many conversations, ever talked about the war.

"Hey," I said, shaking his shoulder lightly. "How come you never told me about Vietnam?"

David shot me a quick look. "I never did?"

"No."

"Huh," he said. A few seconds later, he said, "Shit, man, there isn't that much to tell." And then he changed the subject. "I just can't take the nine to five anymore. It's not real. This is what's real. Just being here. Smell that sage."

"It's nice," I said. But it bothered me that he had just blown off Vietnam again. I felt briefly embarrassed that I would spend so much time talking about my family with Al and yet David wouldn't tell me anything about the war.

I knew that war had to be so much worse than growing up in my family. So wouldn't he need even more to talk about it?

I said, "But the past is real too, right? I mean, how can you just move on without it affecting you?"

"Choices, man. Choices," he said. "We each got to pick what to carry around."

It wasn't like I wanted to be carrying so much around with me. But I didn't see any way to get rid of it so easily.

I felt a little nervous lying there under a sky so big and so full of stars that it made me catch my breath. It was like the entire universe was pressing down on me. We were surrounded by odd rock formations, dramatic black shadows in the twilight, that creeped me out a little. "Won't you get lonely?"

"Of course not. Man, this is what I want. This is my journey and I want to keep moving along it. I was feeling so stuck in that house with so many things weighing me down. I gave my bed to my uncle."

That made me shiver.

He said, "I don't want to be a dentist. Why did I ever think I did? There's not enough time to waste on things that bring us down."

It was hard for me to understand his choice. I *did* want the security of my own place. I *did* want to be surrounded by the nice things I had bought. And I *did* want a job, one that paid well, that I could count on.

"Don't you ever want to get married and have kids?"

He laughed. "No, man. That's just baggage. I need to be free to go wherever is calling me next. You have a kid and then you have to buy things and take the kid to school and make dinner or whatever."

"What about feeling close to someone?"

"Don't you feel close right now? I do. And then the moment will pass. We'll go our separate ways. But we will have been here for it. Then you'll feel close with someone else next week. I'll spend a few days with someone on the road here and there whenever I get lonely. But the fact is we're all in this together and we're all in it alone. Each journey is solitary but we cross paths for company."

His vision made me sad. Always moving from thing to thing. And I was just one thing on the road. What was the point?

"I'm just here, man. I'm just living."

We fell asleep side by side in our individual sleeping bags, as the crickets made a racket.

REINCARNATION

One day over our giant plates of lasagna in one of Al's favorite restaurants, he told me we knew each other from a past life. "I knew that about you the moment I saw you," he said.

"When was it? Like the Middle Ages? Was I a damsel in distress?"

"Ha. You? You've never been a damsel in distress, baby. You've always had the drive to thrive."

"So when?"

"Edo period. Japan, 1600s."

I started laughing. "You've got to be kidding me."

"No. That's one time I know about for sure. There may be others. You were one of the architects of sustainable forest management in modern Japan."

That really got me going. I almost choked on my food.

"I'm not kidding, baby," he said.

"How is it possible that I would be me, today, after having done that then? I don't know anything about whatever it is you just said."

"Because your brain wasn't reincarnated. I'm talking about your soul. The kind of memories you would have would only be of the spiritual wisdom variety, lodged in your soul."

I lit up a cigarette, and he frowned. "When are you going to quit that poison?"

"I guess when I quit all the other poisons I rely on."

"Just do it. You're always putting things off to the future. You never know how much time is left."

"Okay, okay. I promise I'll work on it." I stabbed my fork into the lasagna. "But it sounds like there's plenty of time left because I'll just come back again as someone else."

Al said, "Yup. A cockroach, baby."

I was reminded of my conversation with David in the Badlands, a conversation that was still gnawing at me. I said, "You know, you sound kind of like David. He's always talking about time and how he wants to spend it."

Al's eyebrow went up. "Seems like he's spent a lot of it getting stoned."

"He's searching, I guess." I thought about it some more. "Since he spends so much time searching, even more than me, he must have a lot to figure out."

"But what is he figuring out? I mean, really?"

I ignored Al's comment. "I asked David about whether he ever wants to have a family, and he said something about experiencing moments with different people. It's all fleeting moments for him."

"When he says *moments*, I think I hear him saying *women*. Experiencing different women? Not so bad." He grinned.

"What about your wife, Al?" I was irritated.

"Marge and I have an understanding. She doesn't want physical intimacy any more. It happens to some women at a certain age. But it hasn't happened to me. No sir."

"Duh. I know, Boob."

"So she does her thing and I do mine. What's the problem? We're both okay with it."

I poked holes in the giant noodles.

I guess Al could feel my judgment because he went on. "You know the place she moved to? It's where our daughter lives. Bainbridge Island, up by Seattle. It's beautiful there. She's happy, and I always love going to see them. We have a good time together. We get along great. There's no problem as far as we're concerned."

"Are you sure Marge feels that way too?"

"She says she does, and I have to take her word for it. What am I supposed to do? Stop having physical intimacy when I'm not ready for that?"

The judgmental part of me thought he should but I didn't say that.

What was really bothering me, though, was that he was sounding like David. The rootless life concept made me nervous. It was too close to home. We had always been moving from place to place. Our stuff was always getting lost or thrown out or stolen. Mom was always switching from man to man. I wanted things to stop and stay in place.

"Look, baby," he said, as if he were reading my mind, "nothing on this planet stays the same. Everything, even rocks, are alive, and everything is always moving and changing. You too. Look how different you are from when we first met."

"How?"

"You were just a kid. You were figuring out how to be a waitress. You didn't even know sometimes when I was kidding. You're growing up."

"But that's all moving toward something. Not away."

"Every time you move toward one thing, you're moving away from another. Look, I'm not sorry to see David take off. You're outgrowing him. His choices aren't for you. They're not for me either. Sleeping in a tent? But don't think that you're not growing and changing every moment.

You're turning into a beautiful human." He grinned and added, "Just like me. The only difference between us is that I know I know and you don't know you know."

STUCK IN A RUT

I loved having my own apartment. It was a symbol of how my life was different. I kept it way cleaner than I needed to, especially since I was usually the only one who ever saw it. I couldn't stand any dust bunnies on the floors. I hated clutter. I cleaned my bathroom every day and scrubbed the tub once a week. I kept my clothes, which were all mine and which I didn't have to share with anyone, neatly folded in my dresser, which I had bought at the Salvation Army and scrubbed clean. I had then put contact paper down in each drawer to make sure my clothes didn't have any relationship to the life of whoever had used the dresser before me.

I would wake up feeling safe and calm. I would go to bed alone, having drunk myself to sleep.

So it was a big surprise when one day my Dad showed up at my door.

"Hey, Risé," he said. "Let me in, okay?"

I opened the door a little more, and he pushed it open the rest of the way and marched into my apartment. "Hey, this isn't too bad." He looked around for a second. "Hey, you got something to drink?"

I poured us some gin, and he sat down on the couch. I sat down across the room from him on a wooden chair. He looked slightly disheveled, which was very unusual for him. His cuff lengths were uneven, and there was a stain on the knee of his pants.

"Come over here," he said. But I didn't move. He chugged his drink. "Bonnie left me."

I didn't say anything because I didn't know what to say.

"The whole thing was a misunderstanding. It involved some nonsense with Connie. She blocked her bedroom door with her dresser, and Bonnie got upset about that."

I didn't look at him. In fact, I looked down into my glass. I knew now exactly why Bonnie had left him, and I wanted to scream at him about what he had done to me and what he must have done to those girls all the time, but I couldn't speak.

Dad asked for another drink, so I got up and refilled

his glass, handed it to him, and then returned to my spot across the room.

After a minute, Dad said, "Are you afraid to be alone with me?"

Now I looked at him. "Yes."

What happened next surprised me even more than him showing up on my doorstep. He started weeping, holding his face in his hands, his shoulders heaving. "I'm a sick man, Risé. I'm sick, sick, sick."

Even though he was a sick man, seeing him cry like that almost broke me in half. But I didn't move.

"Why did you do it?"

"Because there's something really wrong with me."

I couldn't disagree. But I couldn't add to the conversation either. It felt too scary.

After a while he said, "Honey, get me another?" and held out his glass. I filled it, he drank it, and he fell asleep on my couch.

I watched him sleeping. All the hardness of his face had fallen away. His wide mouth, which when he was awake was always clenched and taut, softened and relaxed. His forehead, which always had little lines on it like he was concentrating, softened. When he was awake, his big eyebrows, which looked like someone had markered them on his face, gave him a worried look. But now he seemed peaceful. He had just confessed to his crime, and he was like a hairy napping newborn, ready to see what would come next in his life when he woke up and had another drink.

Bonnie came back home after a few days so I thought maybe Dad had taken a hard look at himself and was acting differently, and she had forgiven him. Maybe he did change, for a while anyway, but as I discovered later, it didn't last.

A few years after, Bonnie suffered an aneurysm. She was taken by ambulance to the ICU. By then Connie had left home and was married, which meant Terry was at home alone with Dad.

Terry had gotten a job through one of those work programs for mentally disabled people. One day she told someone at work about what Dad had been doing to her. That evening Dad came home from work and there was a note from the Sheriff's Department telling him that Terry was in foster care. So I knew then that Dad had resumed his old ways.

What was even more upsetting was that after Bonnie returned home from the hospital three months later, the Sheriff's Department let Terry go home too.

ROLFING

I started dating Dale, the owner of the Carrow's Restaurant where I worked. He was legally separated from his wife. He didn't really want much from me, which left lots of evenings and weekends free for drinking. But he did want me for sex, and he was really grateful.

I tried not to burden him with my woes, because I figured that would be a turnoff. But one night in my bed I told him a little about my history. I tried to say it lightly, like it wasn't a big deal. "So I was raped a few times and molested a few more. You'd think I'd have problems with sex, given everything, right?"

He petted my hair. "Those fucking assholes." After a minute he added, "You know, you might benefit from Rolfing."

I started laughing because that sounded like puking, and I couldn't imagine what that would do for me.

But Dale explained how it worked, and I agreed to give it a try.

I made an appointment with the same man who did Rolfing for Dale. When I showed up at his office, he had me sit down at his desk while he explained some things. He was kind of a nerd. He wore little round glasses, and his hair was cut short, military style. He was wearing a Hawaiian print shirt, with big pink flowers all over it. He said Rolfing was about releasing the pain that was trapped in my body's tissues, and I thought about how his shirt looked like the flowers had released pain in pink all over the fabric.

He said, "If you didn't get a chance to let this stuff out at the time, it got stored in your body, like energy." I pictured my body riddled with little bullet holes, each one filled with pain.

He warned me it might be an emotional experience. "When the body finally releases the energy, the emotion associated with the pain also gets released." He added, smiling, "But that's a good thing."

I wasn't sure how good it sounded, but I was willing to give it a try. I stretched out on a table in my underwear, and he began kneading the "soft tissue." It hurt like hell. He dug his fingers into my arms and legs, my shoulders, my neck. It was like I was a dishrag being wrung out by a Russian weightlifter.

For a while I felt like I was going to scream from the pain. Then, as I got used to it, I felt like I was going to cry. But when he started kneading the soft tissue of my upper thigh, I simply lost it.

"Get the fuck off me," I screamed, and jumped off the table, clutching the towel against me.

He said, "Calm down. It's just an energy release." I didn't like being told to calm down, especially by a man who had had his hands on my thigh.

He added, "If you think about it for a second, you'll see that you actually created this."

There were a lot of things I still didn't understand, but I knew that I had not created this, and I felt like punching him in the face. I realize now that what he probably meant was that I hadn't let the pain go, so it was my responsibility that it stayed in my tissue. But at the time it sounded like he was blaming me for the pain. I grabbed my clothes and left.

But Dale talked me through it later that night. "It's probably just too early for you. Maybe you're not ready yet."

The thing is, I was impatient. I wanted to be ready and done with it. I wanted to move on to the butterfly stage.

Dale said, "You know, sex gets better when you can be in the moment and really get into it."

I decided I would make myself ready and go see the Rolfer again. I eventually completed the fourteen-week treatment. Throughout the whole experience, I kept getting flashes of my Dad's face. It was like being electrocuted, and each time the electricity zapped me, my Dad was there controlling the dial.

That's how much I wanted to get better.

GOING TO WORK FOR GOD

Dale divorced his wife, and we lived together for three years. He only drank socially, but I was drinking heavily, and the differences between us, like the varying quantities of alcohol, got to be big. He fell out of love with me, so I went back to living in my own place. I was drunk every night, lonely or having blackout sex, and I kept wetting the bed.

I told a friend who suggested I go and talk with someone named Reverend Shirley Scott. "She's a healer," she said. "Maybe you'll get something out of it."

So I called her office and made an appointment. On the day of my appointment, I drove to her house, which was in a crappy part of town. I locked my car and then checked to make sure it really was locked and crossed the street to her building.

Although she lived in a crappy neighborhood, her home was beautiful. The entrance hall and sitting room were furnished all in white, with gold and glass accents. The room was lit up by large windows accented in silk drapes. The wood floors were covered in fuzzy white rugs. Her assistant walked me down a hall to her study where the Reverend Shirley was sitting on a white wingback chair, apparently just waiting for me.

She was probably in her late 70s. She had a round face, it was a little plump, and she wore her hair neatly and closely cropped. She was wearing expensive-looking gold earrings, a thick gold necklace, and a chunky gold bracelet that stood out against her brown skin. I was sure her blouse had to be one hundred percent silk and probably cost hundreds of dollars. Whoever she was she was making money.

"Hello, dear," she said. "Sit on down."

I mumbled hello back and gave her a nervous smile.

"So why are you here?" she asked rather bluntly.

I hemmed and hawed a little and then admitted that I was wetting the bed.

She said, "I see," and folded her hands across her lap. "Picture someone from your life urinating. You'll need to go back in time."

I started laughing, but at the same time I had a vision of my mother from years earlier. My siblings and I had had friends over and we were sprawled all over the living room furniture. I didn't remember how old I was at the time, but I did remember quite vividly how my mother stood in the doorway, still in the hall, where we all could see her, and dropped her pants. She peed, right then and there on the hallway carpet.

"Come on now," Reverend Shirley said. "Tell me what you're seeing." So I did.

She said, "What was the effect on you of your mother's public peeing?"

"I guess I was embarrassed."

"You guess?"

"I was embarrassed."

"That's right. We're not used to seeing people peeing on the carpeting, and when it's our mother, well, that's worse. I think the ugliness of that incident is why you're wetting the bed. I'm imagining you have some shame about yourself too. That there is the connection."

She had nailed it in about five minutes. I was won over just like that. So I started seeing Reverend Shirley every week.

In our sessions, she always dove right to the point, and I often felt shocked by the things she would tell me, at least until I had had a chance to get used to them. For example, one time she said to me, "Do you know what I see above you? A big fat joint."

Again I started laughing from the surprise. But I stopped quickly as she went on. "The problem with you is that you mindfuck. You smoke pot, then beat yourself up for it, then you smoke pot, then you beat yourself up for it."

That was certainly true.

Another time when I was having frequent headaches, she said, "Look at the parts of the body where your *dis-ease* is." She said it like that to emphasize physical unease. "What trauma is there?"

"In my head?"

"Yes, dear."

"Well my mother used to bang our heads against the wall."

She clicked her tongue. "No. That's not it," she said. "What's in your head?"

"My brain?"

"Hmmmm hnnh." She made a sound that communicated something like, "Yes, of course. Thank God you've caught up with me."

I struggled to figure out what the trauma was to my brain. And then, just like that, I thought and said, "Martin Luther King."

"I beg your pardon?"

"Martin Luther King. We were watching a movie about him in sixth grade."

"Go on."

"My teacher called me up during the movie and told me I had an F."

"That's it then. You decided you were stupid at that moment and that's why your head hurts. You need to believe you are not stupid."

"I'm not. I just, I guess, I feel like maybe I didn't have a good education."

"Did you have a good education?"

"No."

"Was that your fault?"

"Not really."

"Reverend Shirley snapped her fingers and I jumped. "Right here, right now," she said. "Was it your fault?"

"No."

"Are you stupid?"

"No. I'm not stupid."

"Okay then. Your headaches should go away."

And they did.

After about six months of visits, Reverend Shirley decided she was going to move to the very exclusive La Costa neighborhood of San Diego. With her move, she would be one and a half hours away, so I had to cut back on the frequency of our sessions. But I kept going as often as I could make the drive.

On one of my visits, she brought up the smarts issue again. "Remember, dear, how you are, in fact, smart?"

I nodded.

"Well, I need an assistant who has brains. My previous one left. You have told me you are looking for some better work. Come work for me."

I said yes immediately.

I decided I needed to move to the San Diego area as well to save on driving time. I packed up my stuff, broke my lease, and moved everything south in my Celica. I found a condo on the golf course one block away from Reverend Shirley's new place. Every day I went to Shirley's office and helped organize her writings, printed brochures, recruited new followers, scheduled speaking gigs. I went with her on her tours, taking notes on audience members' reactions to what she said. I handed out brochures beforehand. I collected mailing addresses after. I recruited more followers for her.

I was twenty-eight and I felt like this was my calling: to become a minister, or assistant minister, and help people. So I threw myself into the work. I had to answer all phone calls. That was one of my primary responsibilities because Reverend Shirley would never speak directly to any of her clients on the phone. They always had to come to see her and pay for an appointment. Even if someone was begging just "to speak to her for a second," to "run something by her," to "get some quick help for a quick problem," I would have to say she couldn't come to the phone and encourage them to set up an appointment.

Reverend Shirley told me I was doing a good job, although not in so many words. Instead, one day she stood in the doorway to my office and said, "You have earned one hundred dollars more each week." I felt proud and recognized, finally, for what I had dared to believe about myself all along—that maybe I didn't belong in my family.

Reverend Shirley wanted to have her own Church to preach what she called "Christ Consciousness," which was mostly about intentions, visualization, positive thinking, and manifestation. She would tell people to be clear about their intentions, and she always knew when they weren't and would do the finger snap "right here, right now" thing to shake them out of their bullshit. When people said they wanted something, like a better job or a divorce or improved health, she would say, "What do you want? Be specific. A Lamborghini or a Volkswagen? Because God doesn't give a shit either way. You think He can't make it happen? Don't think small."

I started thinking big for the business. I set up group presentations for Reverend Shirley in L.A. That way she could make a whole bunch of money all at once instead of slowly through individual sessions. I started organizing six-week classes in hotel conference rooms with between fifteen and twenty participants per class. Each participant would pay $1500.

I would drive us one and a half hours to L.A. where Reverend Shirley would address the gathered class of mostly young white women, seekers just like me. When it was over, I would drive us back home again.

At night, after a few drinks, I would fall into a heavy sleep, tired from the busy day at work and happy that I was doing something important. I felt like I was working directly for God.

THE HYATT

Even though I soaked up everything Shirley said, I still fell apart every time I went to visit my family in L.A. I would return to San Diego a mess, shaky and exhausted. I was drinking more than ever, and my eyes had huge circles under them. I would cake on makeup to hide the circles.

Reverend Shirley had stopped noticing. She had stopped seeing the trouble I was in, the way she had before.

She had also started to drive me crazy. She and her husband were having some sort of trouble—I could tell from the millions of messages I had to take from him. And attendance was dropping at her talks, which made her cynical. It was the mid-1980s, when the economy was steadily growing and we were getting out of the recession, and I guess people were losing interest in spiritual matters. One day, I tried handing out some of Shirley's brochures to a Tony Robbins seminar crowd gathered at a hotel. A man said, "Does she show you how to make money?"

Shirley's husband started calling me at home too. One day he called thirty times, just to find out where Shirley was.

I finally said, "You have to stop calling me at home," and I wondered why it had taken thirty calls to get me to that point.

At work the next day, Shirley told me she wasn't going to be able to pay me for a while. "The money's dried up," she said. After a pause, she said, "God don't give a shit."

Then she said, "Dear, you got a bag of weed you can sell me?"

At home I called Al.

"I'm sorry, baby, that's happening to you," he said. That made me feel better. He said, "I like Reverend Shirley. But she sure can be a cranky bitch." That made me feel even better.

He added, "Can you get some more work to tide you over?"

I hung up and within two days found myself a bartending job at the Hyatt. It was a good gig because I got to sneak all the drinks I wanted. I was the pool bartender, and most people were blinded by the sun so they couldn't see that for every other drink I poured, I poured myself a quarter glass too.

I would go home from work and drink more, curling up on my couch to read or watch TV. I stopped eating. All my money went to rent, alcohol, and pot.

One day I got the great idea that I needed a vacation, a break from my lonely life. I don't know why, probably the employee discount, but I ended up going to a place that was just like work, the Palm Springs Hyatt. When I got there I put on my bathing suit to head out to the pool. No sooner had I stepped outside than a sand storm hit, pelting my bare skin with BB-sized grains of sand.

Again, I called Al, crying in my hotel room. "I just need to lie out in the sun," I whined.

While we were talking, the storm ended, and Al said, "You like that?" taking credit for changing the weather. I believed him.

He said, "You can come home now," and so I did, leaving Palm Springs, San Diego, and Reverend Shirley behind.

AUDIT

Back in L.A., I restarted my weekly dinners with Al, saw my sisters and my mother when I could, and looked for a job. The first one I landed was Office Manager at Work Wheels, a tire retailer. Next, I worked in an electrician's office.

At these jobs, as usual, I lied, I faked, I played along. But I kept advancing, making more money, and learning all the important things I had missed along the way.

If someone needed an Excel spreadsheet done, I said, "Sure," and then went home and called a friend who might know what the hell that meant. I would find someone who knew how to do the work, and I'd turn it in as mine.

What I found out was that, if I faked it, I would eventually learn it. If I could see what it looked like, I could play the part. When my supervisor bought a Volvo, I went out and bought a Volvo too. If I went to a colleague's house for a party and saw that he had houseplants, then that is what I got for my own home.

The result was a semblance of a life. It all looked the part: my clothes, my hair, my laugh, my résumé. But there was a hole in the middle of it. To dampen the pain of being a ghost in my own life, I drank and I smoked pot. This is how I got by. This is how I made up for all the lost time when no one would teach me anything. I was buying myself time to figure out who I was, later.

I moved into a mobile home with my friend Michelle. At home in the evenings, as I worked through bottle after bottle of booze, I took stock of my life. I had nice furniture. I had a good car. My teeth were fixed. My nails were nice. I was a good gift giver, picking out the perfect thing for the perfect occasion for my friends or family. I had some nice throw pillows. My home was clean. I looked successful.

I also made a to-do list:
- Have sex sober.
- Get married, have kids.

My list made me depressed. Reverend Shirley would have said I wasn't having enough intention. And then I got much more depressed when a doctor diagnosed me with cervical cancer. I followed up with second and third opinions. By the time I was done looking for the right answer, five doctors had diagnosed me with cancer.

I told Michelle, and then at dinner with Al that week I told him too.

He was quiet. "I know an appropriate joke," he said, "but I'll spare you."

"Thank you."

I said, "How can I be so sick when things are so much better than they used to be? How come I don't feel good?"

"You mean in spite of having cancer?"

"I mean emotionally."

Al thought about if for a minute. Then he said, "So I knew this guy, a gynecologist, and he was unhappy at work. He wanted to do something else with his life. His brother, who had an old car in his garage he wanted fixed, selfishly suggested that he become an auto mechanic, and my friend thought that was a good idea. He applied to a training school, got in, and went through the whole program. The final exam consisted of taking apart an engine and rebuilding it."

I said, "Is this the joke?"

"Just listen. So my friend did the exam and waited for his results. He was shocked when his instructor told him he had passed with flying colors. He scored 150 percent on the exam.

"My friend said to the instructor, 'How can this be? I've never heard of getting 150 percent on a test.'

"The instructor said, 'Well, half the test was scored on disassembling the engine. You got a full 50 percent on that. The other half was for the rebuilding and, again, you got the full 50 percent. You did an amazing job, very impressive.' He then said, 'I gave you an additional 50 percent for doing it all through the muffler.'"

I got the joke but I didn't get how it applied to me.

Al said, "Maybe you're doing it wrong. You're using your old way of doing things to do something new."

That made sense. I hadn't updated my strategies. I told that to Michelle later that night, and she suggested we try Scientology. I thought maybe it was my chance to find a new approach to solving my life.

So we went to the orientation. The Scientologists taught us that current behavior is strongly affected by past experiences, and the memory of those past experiences can lead to irrationality. What they called the *reactive mind* is the part of our brains that simply responds without consciousness to that memory. My goal, they told me, was to learn to rid myself of the unwanted influence of the reactive mind so that I could achieve life in a rational state, always doing what was in the best interest of my survival. Clear your mind, they said, and you can become your truest, best self.

I figured it couldn't hurt. It seemed that, no matter how hard I tried, I couldn't clear away the crap from the past that I was hauling around.

Michelle and I signed up for a twenty-one-day purification rundown to help us on the way toward rationality. On the first day, the Scientologists gave us each 100 milligrams of Niacin and then told us to run on a treadmill.

I changed into running shorts and a T-shirt, stretched, and started out at a slow pace. But it was a beautiful day and the sun, just on the other side of the floor-to-ceiling windows, made me feel impatient, and I started running faster. I thought about my family and how I was running away from them and succeeding, leaving them all behind.

After about ten minutes of running, my head and neck started tingling—more like prickling—and then I felt like I had been set on fire, turning bright red. I guessed that my impurities were so intense that I had almost combusted when getting them out.

Next, they had us head into the sauna to complete the process. Michelle, who had done the reading, explained that the Niacin had dilated our blood vessels, sending blood throughout our bodies. The sweating would be the last step in getting the impurities out.

Suddenly, while we were sitting in there baking, an old sunburn appeared on my skin, the bikini marks and all. Michelle said, "Look" and pointed. I recognized the burn as the one from years earlier when Rochelle and I had driven to the beach, slathered ourselves in oil, and quietly fried, while we drank some cheap Margarita mix out of a jar. That's when I had told her about Dad and Robert. She had hugged me, said "Yeah, me too," and then quickly jumped up to get a burger from the snack shop.

I even noticed the prints from the little bows at the corners of my bikini bottom. It was like my body was a piece of film and it had recorded everything I had seen and heard and experienced my whole life. This was going to be a major problem for me, I realized, because destroying that many images was going to take forever.

I followed up the day's purification with a trip to the market, where I picked up a bottle of rum and a six pack of Coke.

PISSING ON MYSELF

I astonished the hell out of my doctors when they discovered my cancer was gone. "How did you do it?" they wondered. I told them about the Scientology audit process.

The Scientologists meanwhile were pressuring Michelle and me to join what they called their Sea Organization, which was like their religious order. The way they described it was kind of how I pictured the navy, with uniforms and admirals. Some of the people lived on ships so they could travel all over the world. The part that appealed to me was the part about daily audits and training and then helping people. The part I didn't like was that they wanted me to work in the anti-drug education campaign. I felt unqualified.

I talked about it with Al and found out that he and Ken had been part of Scientology a while back. About joining the Sea Org, he was unusually blunt: "No fucking way," he said. At home Michelle talked about how we could see the world, traveling on one of the Scientologist's luxury ships.

Meanwhile, at the Church of Scientology of Los Angeles, my trainers kept pushing me to stop getting drunk. I would do an audit, and they would tell me I hadn't stopped. I would agree, and then they would make me run for several hours at a time. It felt like a punishment but they called it a purification.

So I eventually quit Scientology. Not because Al didn't want me to do it. Not because I didn't want to do it, because I sort of did. But because I could not stop getting drunk.

After Scientology, I worked myself into an even better life. Even though I was trashing my body every day with drugs and alcohol, I kept pulling my way up from job to better job. I talked my way into a $75,000-a-year salary, which I only lost when my boss found out I had basically no relevant job experience whatsoever. At another job, I slept my way into a promotion when my married boss noticed some of my non-work-related attributes.

And then I landed a job at Sealy, supervisor of sales, the best job I'd ever had. Now I could afford the best of everything, and from the outside I looked like I had won. I had beaten the odds, made myself into something when everything in my early life had thrown up walls, had tripped me up, had yanked me backwards. My friends congratulated me by buying me drinks.

But I still felt empty.

Around my thirtieth birthday, soon after getting the job, I met Chris at a Sealy trade show. He was super skinny and had a shy smile and soft blond hair that fell partly over his eyes, and he seemed to like everything about me. "Hey," he said, "I saw you at your booth, earlier."

I had noticed him too. But all I said was, "Okay."

"Just that, you know, I noticed you, and um...," he trailed off into soft laughter and rolled his eyes.

"What?"

"You're definitely already married or you've got some guy, for sure, right?" That's when he looked at me directly for the first time.

"If you're trying to ask me out, you should probably just get to the point."

"Okay. Yes, I am. You have an awesome smile."

"Meet me in the hotel bar at four."

Chris was the most attentive man I had ever met, and it drove me crazy. But I wanted a change. I had never been in a healthy relationship, and it was one of the items on my to-do list. Even though I was not physically attracted to him, he was cute and that combined with me feeling sorry for him convinced me to let him take me out for dinner.

As I always did when men took me out, I felt obligated to have sex with him. He was so grateful and appreciative that I was almost embarrassed.

"You don't get out much, do you?" I asked.

"Not with girls like you. You're so hot."

My ego desperately needed stroking, so I put up with him for a few weeks. The weeks turned into months. He moved from Sacramento where he had worked in another mattress company's warehouse. He quickly found himself a new warehouse job in L.A.

Chris provided me with excellent pot, which we smoked every day, and our combined incomes bought us a lot of alcohol. So I accepted his marriage proposal, with a wedding date far off in the distance, and we moved into an apartment together.

We headed off to our different jobs in the mornings. At night I drank myself into a stupor, which was one way I avoided having sex with him on our Sealy mattress.

If I drank enough I would fall asleep on the couch. I had started up with the nighttime peeing again—I would pee myself and the couch because I was too wasted to wake up and walk to the bathroom. I knew what Reverend Shirley would have said about it, but I ignored her voice in my head. Chris, on the other hand, would just beg me to get up and use the toilet one time before I fell into a deep sleep for the night. "You're going to wet the couch. Please, Risé."

I would hit him and scream at him, like a caged weasel. "Leave me alone," I would yell. "Leave me the fuck alone."

He would make me a lunch for work and he always put a note in it. Like he would write, "You are my sunshine" or "Want to see a movie tonight?" The notes just made me feel guilty, so I would flush them down the toilet at work.

He'd wash my car for me on the weekends. Every morning he'd pull it out of the garage and start it for me when I had to go out. He would turn on the seat warmers so my butt wouldn't get chilled.

I hated him for all of it, and I hated myself for hating him. He helped himself to my abuse like it was free nuts at the bar, and he just didn't get that the cost of the nuts was more than covered by the cost of the alcohol. Every day, his goal was to make me happy.

The harder he tried, the less respect I had for him. Al pointed out the irony. "You get that it's kind of pathetic that you hate him for loving you, right?"

"Shut up," I said. I felt what I felt.

After three years of postponing our wedding, I broke things off. I felt like I had failed on purpose.

PARALYSIS

During my relationship with Chris, after we got engaged, I told Al he had to walk me down the aisle. Then when I broke up with Chris I figured Al would walk me down the aisle to marry someone else when the time came. But Al, who was inconsistent with his blood pressure medication, suffered a stroke, which meant that he would never be able to. It left him partly paralyzed, so he moved up north to live with his wife Marge.

In 1989 when I was thirty-two, I flew up to Bainbridge Island to visit. Despite everything I had heard about

Seattle, it was not raining. As the plane circled around the city before landing, sunlight reflected off the wings and the top of the Space Needle. I caught a cab to the waterfront where I took the ferry across the Sound to the island. Seagulls drifted alongside the boat, and some people tossed French fries into the air so they could catch them. The sunlight caught the tops of gentle waves on the water.

Bainbridge was semirural, sleepy, a combination of farms, forests, and beachfronts. The boat headed into the harbor past yachts and sailboats and kayakers. Marge met me at the ferry terminal. She was a little plumper than the last time I'd seen her and dressed very differently—wearing jeans, a checkered blouse, and tennis shoes. Her gray hair was pulled back into a ponytail. She threw her arms around me and said, "We are so excited you're here."

On the drive to her home, we had to stop for a golden retriever napping in the middle of the road. Marge honked and we waited for the dog to get up and slowly walk to the side so we could pass.

Bainbridge was the opposite of Los Angeles—still versus frenetic. The roads were nearly empty. It wasn't exactly quiet—birds were yammering constantly and bees and hummingbirds were buzzing and zipping all over the place—but the noise was so different from the sound of traffic and construction I was used to that I felt a little nervous. It was like time was moving at a different pace, and the rest of the world was happening somewhere else and had no effect here.

Marge turned between two fir trees down a long driveway to a wood house sitting in the clearing. "He's changed," she warned me as she put on the emergency brake.

She was right. Al, who had been awarded a Purple Heart for his service, who had a black belt in karate, was now shriveled and bent and small. He was sitting on a recliner, covered in a blanket that nearly swallowed him up. He could barely speak—one half of his mouth couldn't move. And he had trouble holding up his head.

I hugged him carefully and held his hand. His eyes were shining. I tried to hide the fact that I was crying. He wagged one finger at me and said something that I couldn't understand.

During the week of my visit, Marge and I did most of the talking, and I came to understand that Al was right about her. She was strong enough that she would have been okay with their arrangement. She was strong enough to care for him.

Every day we walked through the woods behind their house to a little convenience store with old, warped wooden floors. It smelled like pickled something or other. Marge would buy herself a bottle of wine and I would get a six pack of beer. We spent the evenings drinking on the back deck or watching TV next to Al who was usually napping. During the day, Marge took me to the beach or out to lunch. When Al was awake, I read the newspaper to him and chatted about the world and about life. His eyes told me what I needed to know—whether he was tired or listening or confused.

The whole time I was there I kept thinking about what Al had told me about how everything alive is always changing. It was like his change made me more aware of my own—and the ways I still needed to. At night, listening to the hooting of some type of owl out in the woods, I thought about how nothing stays the same, even though when I was younger it felt like the bad things lasted forever. I was, on the outside at least, the person I had always wanted to be: strong, independent, successful. But on the inside, I still felt a lot of the time like the little girl who had been pried open by her brother and father. The little girl who couldn't outwrestle or outsmart her own mother. And now my friend Al, who had become my parent in my young adult years, was pretty much gone, leaving me alone again and needing to figure out on my own what would come next.

At the end of the week, I gave him a hug and kissed the top of his head. I figured this would be the last time we would see each other, at least in this lifetime. He had taught me enough about his belief in past lives that I was sure we'd see each other again somewhere else.

On the ferry ride back to the city, I stayed up on the top deck where I could hide in a corner, mostly unseen by anyone but the seagulls. I remembered the time I had gone to dinner with Al at an Italian restaurant in Manhattan Beach. I had had too much to drink, and I excused myself to go to the bathroom. On the way, I passed a pay phone and made the decision to call my boyfriend at the time.

I was horny and tried to convince him to drive the one and a half hours from his home to pick me up. When we finally hung up, I returned to the table and Al had left. I looked at my watch and saw that I had been gone for more than half an hour.

I called him. He didn't mince words. "That was crap," he said. "Show some class."

So those disappointing words were ringing in my head. My shame over drinking.

Then I remembered his admonition from years earlier: "Stop trying so hard, baby. Just have the intention and let things happen for you." I stopped trying not to cry and gave myself over to it.

CALL-IN RADIO

Dr. David Viscott was a radio show host. He had the softest voice. I loved it—it was calm, thick, and blunt with a Boston accent, kind and direct. He was a psychologist who would counsel people over the air. He had the gift of being able to pinpoint exactly what the problem was after just a few conversational exchanges. His radio show came on in the afternoons on KABC, and no matter what else I had to do, I always made sure to listen.

On April 13 of 1990, I took my lunch break in my car so I could listen to Viscott's show. I was thirty-three.

In my Volvo, I turned up the volume.

A man called in to the show. He said, "I'm a writer and I'm blocked."

Viscott said, "Hey, man, have you had a drink today?"

"Why are you asking?" the writer said.

"Just answer me." I felt nervous. I leaned in to hear.

The writer said, "I've had a couple beers."

Viscott said, "You're an alcoholic."

It was crazy. How could he know the caller was an alcoholic from that exchange? But I wasn't even focusing on how crazy that was. I was focusing on something else. I was thinking, "If I called Dr. Viscott, what would he say to me?"

And I knew the answer. I suddenly could not not know it anymore.

That night after work, as if to prove the point, I got drunk and had a blackout. In the morning, at seven, I smoked a joint at the breakfast table while I was talking with my roommate Cathy, my best friend at the time. I said to her, "I'm an alcoholic."

She said, "Uh, yeah."

So I got dressed and marched out to my car and drove to my Mom's house. I knocked. She had by then been sober about sixteen years. As soon as she opened the door, right there in the hallway, I said, "I'm an alcoholic." She immediately started doing an infuriating happy dance.

"I told you, I told you, I told you," she sang, raising her fist triumphantly into the air.

Irritated, I returned home and took all my drugs and all my alcohol and flushed everything down the toilet. Then I went to the shelf in the living room and pulled out the book an old boyfriend had given me. He had inscribed it on April 14 of 1976. It was The Big Book for alcoholics. I'd never once opened it. Not for fourteen years, to the exact day.

SOBERING UP

Getting sober was a lot harder for me than making money. It is the hardest thing I have ever done.

Not drinking was like walking through life with your fingertips cut off. The raw nerves were exposed and I felt everything, like it was the first time. I had never cleaned my house sober before. The smell of the scouring powder made me woozy. The shine off the mirror was a glare. Everything hurt.

I tried calling Reverend Shirley, but her new assistant wouldn't let me speak with her. She said, "You need to make an appointment." I hung up.

I had never gone grocery shopping without getting high first. The colors of the vegetables and fruits were so intense I had to hide in the bread aisle with its browns and tans until the feeling passed.

People looked different, uglier. They weren't as funny. Television shows made me cry or furious. Everything I saw or touched blinded or zapped me, and I lived life terrified about what might give me a jolt next. Sounds were harsh and sharp. Every shape had an edge.

A friend tried to get me to drink. "It'll calm you down."

But I couldn't. I said, "I can't. It's been twenty-one days and thirteen hours. I don't want to have to start all over." I imagined my fingertips being ripped off again.

Over time, I realized, you would get more and more used to it, but your fingertips would never grow back. It would always hurt to touch anything.

By the time we started going to AA together, Mom had graduated college with honors and a degree in Business Administration. She had taken the money she won in her lawsuit against Dad and bought herself a boob job. Even though she weighed 100 pounds, the doctor gave her a D cup, and I was always afraid she was going to fall over from the weight.

Meanwhile, I was a sobriety virgin, and I had lost my best friend, alcohol, the thing that had gotten me through so much pain, right about the same time I had lost my friend Al. I stopped wearing makeup and yanked my hair back into a severe ponytail, shields against attention, and cried myself to sleep at night.

My mother said, "Just because things are hard on the inside, you don't want to give up altogether on the outside."

At AA, people who knew my mother would come up to me and tell me how much she loved her children.

Mom, who was dating someone new and seemed happy for once, said, "You have turned into such a bitch that I am going to start an AA group for mothers of bitches."

I said, "But it's really hard."

"You don't know what hard is."

After I got sober, Mom agreed to go to therapy with me. We saw the same therapist Mom had made us all see briefly back when I was a teenager. We tossed around some old crap with the therapist who knew our history quite well. I started to see some good things about Mom now that she wasn't drinking, all things that had been buried under her rage and frustration. In therapy she let out her humor a few times, and I saw how quick she was. One time she pointed at me and said, "I want things too, you know." I saw how in some ways we were alike.

She bought each of us kids a copy of the book *You Can't Afford the Luxury of a Negative Thought*. I had a little trouble accepting the gift without wincing—

maybe right then and there affording myself a luxury I shouldn't have.

With our relationship patched a little by therapy, Mom and I went shopping together occasionally, and we found things to laugh about, but we never grew close. Whenever I spent time with her she would resort to some of her old ways, trying to get me to do things for her, and I never trusted her enough to feel at ease.

One time she said, "Honey, no man with money will ever want you."

Another time over the phone I asked her, "Am I pretty?"

There was a long pause, and then she said, "Well, really, it's your personality."

THE LADDER

Now that I wasn't drinking, I could think more clearly. I saw that, compared to most people, I was doing really well. I felt like I was becoming the success I had initially pretended to be. Compared to my family, I was in another stratosphere.

The disparity between us wasn't just because I was doing better. It was also because my siblings were doing much worse.

Rochelle, who had stayed sober for twenty years, suddenly started using again. She and her daughter Arlene, who was pregnant, started doing drugs together. Then Rochelle divorced her husband whom she had met in AA. Soon after she was diagnosed with diabetes. She had a terrible case of it and required three insulin injections a day. In 2003, she suffered what doctors called "a psychotic break" and had to be admitted to a psychiatric hospital.

Rhonda, who had stopped using drugs at nineteen, started using again after being sober for fifteen years. She gradually became more and more dysfunctional, neglecting to pay her bills or listen to phone messages. In her forties, she got pregnant, using drugs and barely eating during the whole nine months, until she gave birth to an autistic son.

Renee started using drugs at the age of ten. At seventeen, she gave birth to a son. Eventually she lost custody because of her drug use. Fourteen years later, she was still selling drugs and turning tricks out of her mobile home. She had a second boy by then, nine years old. When the kid's father found out about her prostitution, she lost custody of him too.

By the time I got sober, Robert was homeless. One day he showed up at my door with a bloody shirt and a blown-up lip. I called Rhonda who thought the solution was to come over with a fifth of booze. So I decided we would drive him to the hospital where he got stitched up. Raymond showed up at the hospital too. None of us wanted to take Robert home, so Raymond told a nurse that Robert needed to be admitted to the sixth-floor rehab recovery unit. We left him there, feeling guilty. On our way across the parking lot, a nurse came out and started yelling at us, which made the feeling worse.

Another time Robert rode his bike to my back door. He said he had a flat tire. I wouldn't let him in, but I gave him a bag of groceries. I found out he was living under an underpass and pushing around his belongings in a red shopping cart.

Raymond was less of a train wreck than the rest of my brothers and sisters. He was really good looking and kind of an asshole, but he had a good job. And when he got married, he calmed down and got nicer. He and his wife even took in Robert for a while.

Henry was on and off drugs and in and out of prison. The longest he was sober was for nine months.

Lisa had met a guy at sixteen and instantly gotten pregnant. He joined the Air Force and they had moved away to Montana, and we were all disconnected from her.

Bonnie had gone insane. Ever since she had found out about what Dad had done to her daughters, she had stopped leaving the house. Every day she sat on the couch in her nightgown watching televangelists. If you talked to her, her eyes would glaze over and she would smile.

When my brothers and sisters would visit me, I would see them looking at my better clothes, my manicured nails, my gradually improving cars, my clean furniture and landscaped yard. I saw them, and I knew they thought that, just like it was when we were little, we all were supposed to suffer together. What belonged to one belonged to all. What didn't belong to all belonged to no one.

Every time I felt myself ascending some sort of metaphoric ladder, I could feel them all pulling me back down. I'd be on my way to work and Rhonda would call to tell me Rochelle had a heart attack. Or Robert would call to borrow money. Someone would get sick or get fired or get pregnant.

Every time they called I felt compelled to stop whatever I was doing and run to help or give them money or make a hospital visit. But I still kept myself at a distance deep in my heart.

The past clung to us like a fine dust. If you tried to blow it off, it would lift temporarily and then settle back on.

UNSENT LETTERS

When I was in my early twenties, I had written my Dad a jumbled, confusing, mixed-message letter:

Father, hi. I would love for both of us to sit down and talk about this. There are so many questions I would like to have answered. Do you realize how sick you are? I have so much hate for you and I need to get it out. I wish you were not my father. I have so tried to block it out of my head.

That little episode when you came upstairs, you

came into my room and played around with me,
your daughter. Is that how you care for your
children? I thought it was Robert who also had a
habit of visiting my room every once in a while.
I feel so guilty about feeling good.
Stop fucking with Connie and Terry. I feel so much
empathy for them.
When you left all of us did you ever think what an
effect you would have?

But I never sent it. Now that I was sober, I wrote him again, this time more to the point: "Dad, I want you to know I forgive you for being an alcoholic and screwing up your life and mine." I never sent that one either.

Then a few months later, I called him and said, "I am so done with you. You have ruined my life."

He said happily, "Everything's fine." He told me they had let Robert out of jail, and so Robert had stolen a friend's bike and ridden all the way to Hemet, the town where Dad and Bonnie lived. "We're barbecuing steaks."

I said, "Don't ever call me again" and hung up.

Five days later, the morning after I got my five-month sobriety coin, Rhonda's husband telephoned. "Dad is dead," he said. At first I thought he meant his dad. But he clarified. "No, yours."

It was impossible. My father's gigantic will alone should

have kept him going for at least another twenty years. He was only fifty-eight.

"No way," I said. "You guys are always so dramatic."

"Risé, it's true. No drama here. Robert called."

I felt a gnawing in my stomach. But I still didn't believe it. Instead, I called my father's house. Bonnie answered. Robert was screaming in the background. I could hear her saying to him, "Oh, Robert, Dad is fine. He's fine."

So everything was fine, I told myself. I called the hospital to get the details. The doctor got on the phone right away and told me they had pronounced my father dead. "It was a heart attack," he said.

I was two and a half hours away from Hemet. In a daze, I left my house and went out to my car. I turned the key and sat there in the driveway, idling, muttering over and over, "I'm sorry. I'm sorry."

Dad's and Bonnie's house in Hemet was a mobile home surrounded by plastic flowers, which threw me since Dad had always loved gardening. When I walked in, I saw that Bonnie's condition had obviously worsened. She was on the couch next to a trash bag filled with soiled diapers. "Your Dad's in the bedroom," she said cheerfully.

The house was a mess. There were newspapers all over the floor and food containers left on the kitchen counters. The steaks my father had said they were barbecuing were in the fridge being eaten by cold-stunned flies.

I found Robert in Dad's bedroom, sitting on the mattress, which was in the middle of the room, on the floor, askew, without a frame. The rest of the floor was covered with cigarette butts, whiskey bottles, and beer cans. Nothing was hung in the closet. All of Dad's clothes were in a heap. My father had always been so meticulous, and I couldn't mesh this new vision of him with my old one.

Robert was jingling a mess of coins in his pocket. He had shaved one-half of his face. "Risé," he said. "Dad died yesterday."

"No, Robert," I corrected him. "He died today."

"Oh." He jingled the coins more.

I plopped down on the mattress too, next to my messed-up brother. Life was weird. The last time we had been on a mattress together, I had been trembling in fear, praying for him to go away. But now I was the strong one, and my brother was nervously jingling coins, half shaved.

I figured out what to do. I started by cleaning up the bedroom, pointing Robert in the direction of the bathroom and telling him to shower. Rochelle showed up within the hour and together we cleaned the house and took Bonnie's diapers to the trash cans. Then we sat down to go through their bills and pay them. I called Connie and told her she needed to come home and figure out what to do about Bonnie and Terry. I called the funeral home and made arrangements for Dad's burial.

On the way home the next day, I kept reviewing all the things we had taken care of. I kept thinking, "The mess is cleaned up." But I didn't feel relief. Mostly, I felt sorry.

ONE MORE DAY

Time and again, I was tempted to drink. One time a Wilson Phillips song literally instructed me to "Hold on for One More Day," and so I did. But I felt alone and empty. I hung on, focusing on work and AA meetings. I went six times a week. For my first sobriety anniversary a new AA friend bought me a Barbie, my very first doll, and I put it on my bookshelf, like it was a trophy.

I found out that two people had filed sexual harassment suits against Dad before he died, and that made me want to drink. Then one day I learned from Rhonda that Dad's heart attack happened while he and Robert were having sex with a prostitute on the dirty mattress on the floor. I even got in my car to drive to the liquor store when I heard that. But I made myself walk back inside the house.

I used a delay tactic I had come up with. It went like this: I would never tell myself I couldn't drink. That would simply have made me want to rebel. Instead, I would coax myself to hold on for another twenty-four hours. "You can drink tomorrow," I would tell myself every day.

At AA, I would stand up and share stories about the times I had stolen things, hit people, been raped, lied. The more I owned up to these shameful things the less I felt like they had a hold on me. It was like I was shedding them. I talked every opportunity I had. "I am an alcoholic. I stole pills. I drank at work. I peed the couch." I talked and talked, throwing down the stories like they were bread crumbs that would help me find my way back to my real self. For every hour I had listened to the people around me, trying to learn from them how to live, I needed to talk five more.

Over time I began practicing what I called the "responsible withhold," meaning I would spare people my need to talk when there was the danger I might overwhelm them. Not everyone was like Al, capable of listening so well and so much. I recognized that, with my need to talk, I might blow people out like candles on a birthday cake.

After Dad died, I was so miserable, torn apart with guilt

and terrible confusion about what was my responsibility and what wasn't, that I started plotting how to kill myself. I had to do it in a responsible way, one that didn't make a mess or burden anyone, and it is very hard to come up with a method that won't cause a problem. A gunshot sends blood and brain parts everywhere. Jumping off something leaves a mess at the bottom, and it's too scary anyway. Drowning yourself forces people to conduct expensive searches for your body. Walking in front of a bus traumatizes the driver and all the riders. Even taking pills, which you'd think would be so considerate, makes you empty your bowels, and people often find you before you're dead.

I kept picturing Renee having to strip my bed and wash my sheets, and that always made me pause. Then I would picture my mother's face, and there was something about it, something shiny, like triumph. If I got that far that would usually make me stop too. But if I went past that point in my head, then I would crank the music, grabbing on to each lyric like it was a life ring: "Don't you know things'll change/Things'll go your way."

At AA, people would say about suicide, "You don't want to leave before the miracle." For me that became a little joke: I didn't think there was going to be any kind of miracle, so saying that always made me crack up, and sometimes the joke itself was what kept me holding on, the fact that I was in on it. "Hey, Risé," I would laugh, "don't want to leave yet. You might miss the fucking miracle."

I was the fucking miracle, I thought. The fact that I was still alive.

TINK

I was three years sober when a friend of mine told me I needed to attend a class that this "amazing woman" was teaching at a house in Manhattan Beach. So I went.

About fifteen other people and I sat down on folding chairs that had been arranged in the home's living room. Five minutes after the class was supposed to start, a large woman wearing a blue shirt, cotton pants, and tennis shoes entered the room and said, "Hey, everyone. I'm Tink."

She asked everyone to tell a little about themselves, while she paced back and forth, saying only "Great" after each person spoke and then gesturing at the next one.

A lot of the people seemed to know her already and I noticed that they made a point of stressing their special connection with her. "I met Tink at . . . " "Tink and I go back . . ." "Tink saved me from . . ." It was weird, but I remember feeling jealous that I didn't know her already.

When we were all done with introductions, this woman who was the focus of so much respect, said, "Okay, well, we'll start by talking about what kind of a being you are. There are three types."

She explained that a love-oriented being is all about bonding experiences, sharing, and comforting. That type of person looks at things in terms of how people are relating. While she talked softly, she moved her hands gently from side to side, I guess to show what a love-oriented person was like. "They get accused of being too sentimental, too emotional," she cooed.

I thought, "That has to be me."

"A causation-oriented being," she now said, "is about producing, action, success. Forward motion. Alright?" She was punching one hand into the palm of the other. "When upset, these people don't like to be touched."

I revised my self-image. Clearly, I was cause oriented.

The third type of person, she explained, is communication and understanding-oriented. Their goal in life is to understand and to be understood. They tend to be anxious, uncertain, and to seek out information.

That had to be who I was, I decided.

Tink then explained that we all have some of these elements in us and that people are more or less balanced among the three types. When people are strongly one type of person, then they run into trouble. I wondered what happened if a person was strongly all three types.

Lynn then acted out husband-wife scenarios in which the husband and wife were different types and had trouble relating to each other.

"Honey, we're going to be late. We need to get there in ten minutes."

"Oh, sweetheart, do you like the dress I bought for the occasion?"

"What you're wearing doesn't matter. We need to leave now."

"I'm just trying to make you proud of the way I look. Don't you care?"

I couldn't imagine what kinds of husbands and wives would talk to each other so nicely.

She went on to describe the mechanics of each of the three types of people. For example, the mechanics of love include reassurance, hugging, and gift giving.

The mechanics of cause include setting goals, taking responsibility, making a schedule. And the mechanics of understanding include listening, prioritizing, formulating concepts, and trying to resolve issues.

Tink said, "So we need to understand the type of person we are interacting with." She acted out her husband-wife scenarios again, this time with the spouse understanding these types.

The idea was that you would respond to the person in the way they could actually hear. So you'd reassure or hug the love-oriented person. You'd agree on a specific time and plan of action with the cause-oriented person. Maybe you'd sit down and do research with the understanding-oriented person. And then everyone would feel satisfied with the outcomes. Everyone would succeed.

My mind was blown by this woman who was explaining the world in a way I had never heard before. She was making sense of my family and giving me a tool set for dealing with them. My mother was cause-oriented. I guessed Dad had been love-oriented except that he was so messed up that a hug was never enough.

Her whole system was showing me how I could get along with my family.

By the end of the evening, I was in awe, and I was sure I had found a new teacher. We became instant friends.

Tink was a bundle of contradictions. I found out that

she read ferociously, but she was no bookworm, and her favorite activity was to be outside, with dogs. Plus, she had a fifth-degree black belt in karate. She wanted to be an actress and had even appeared in a few B movies in the late sixties, but she was too grounded and sensible to take herself seriously on screen. Although she was an athlete, she was overweight and loved to eat.

She had one foot solidly planted in this world and a wing flying in another.

Every week I went to see her for Guiding sessions. We would sit across from each other at her desk. The sessions began with what Tink called TMA, for Tell Me About It. She would say to me, "I haven't seen you in a week. What's been happening?"

I would start talking about whatever was going on with me or whatever I was thinking. The whole time Tink would be taking notes in one of her many notebooks.

Tink would ask me questions to help me get to the emotion of whatever it was I was focusing on, like being raped. She might say, "What did the room smell like? What were you feeling?" We would "run" a troubling incident several times, with more and more detail each time. Tink would say, "Make it bigger." She would push me to go deeper and deeper, so I could get better.

The session would continue until Tink felt I had moved up a level from where I had started. There were many levels, such as Death, Apathy, Despair, Hopelessness, and Doubt. No matter where I came in, I had to move up a level, or we would keep on going until I had.

When I was finally done, no matter how long it took, whether an hour or four, Tink would Acknowledge. She would say, "Oh, wow, that must have been terrible" or whatever was appropriate, and the whole time I felt like no one existed in the world but me and her.

It was like she was Rolfing my soul.

And when we'd hit the GEP, or Good Ending Point, Tink would simply announce the session was over and say, "This is a good place to end."

She told me that my number-one downfall was a lack of self-esteem, both in this and past lives. She set about rebuilding me, turning me back into the true person I was.

BACK AROUND TO GO

Tink and I also spent just as much time together as friends. We went out to eat all the time. We took our dogs to Palos Verdes in Tink's old station wagon, which she called Horse. During our long walks, we would talk about politics or concerts or movies. We went to Hawaii and Tahiti together, always searching for the perfect sand, the perfect sunset, the perfect ocean view.

Tink hardly ever talked about herself, and my biggest revelation about her was when I saw her with her own family, how they all hugged and adored each other.

When I'd put myself down, she'd gently chastise me: "Don't ever belittle yourself. Don't dwell on negatives." She would call me at work with a command to have fun. "Today is the last day for the electrical show at Disneyland."

"But I have to work."

"It's the very last day for the show."

"What about work?"

"We need to see the show."

So we went.

I frequently talked to Tink about my addiction. I told her how I had become dysfunctional when I stopped drinking. I had even let my nails go, something that for me had always been a sign of the state of someone's health.

Tink shocked me one day when we were playing Monopoly. I was winning, and I had Park Place, Broadway, the purple properties, and all the red ones. I drew a Chance card, one that showed the rich guy as a hobo. I imagined him as a drunk homeless person. "Of course I would draw this one," I said.

Tink said, "Alcohol saved your butt. If you hadn't drunk your way through your teens and twenties, you wouldn't have survived your family."

"Well then why did I need to stop?" There was a part, just a small part, that secretly hoped Tink was going to tell me that it wasn't bad for me to drink. I could start up again and feel good about it.

But she didn't. "It saved you at first, but then it became a problem too. So you had to stop. But then when you stopped, then the stopping became a problem."

Everything she said sounded so like the most obvious truth in the world that I wondered why I hadn't thought it first myself.

I shared with her my most shameful moments. Like when I had a one-night stand with someone I met in a bar. We had sex and then I needed to use the bathroom. I returned to the bed, and he said, "Don't you wash your hands when you go to the bathroom?"

Tink said, "Why do you feel shame?"

"Because I should have known better."

"Why?"

"What do you mean?"

"Why should you have known better?"

"Because it's something people know."

"It's not something you knew or you would have done it."

She dismantled years and years of my muddled thinking just like that, easily, just by talking with me.

She took me to get my first dog. I was thirty-six. We spent six months visiting shelters. Tink would teach me what to look for, whether the dogs were more love-oriented or wanted to have their own space. I ended up choosing a Yorkie whom I named Abby. She was understanding-oriented and would turn her head to the side when I talked to her, as if to hear me better.

I continued my talking streak, now directing most of it at Tink. One time after I had been talking for about two hours straight, I said, "Oh god. I am so sorry. I've sucked up all the air in the room with my blabbing."

Tink shouted, the first and only time I ever heard her do it: "Stop it. Stop saying you're sorry."

I wanted to apologize for that too, but she had scared me and I bit my tongue. That is until I started talking again.

When my father's old house went on the market, I decided to go back and "run" the scenes I had stuck in my head. It was the house where Dad had molested me. Tink had promised she would be on the phone with me the whole time I was there, but I couldn't get the phone to work, so I had to handle it on my own.

I walked into our old bedroom. It was smaller and even dingier than I had remembered. I couldn't imagine how we had all fit in there. I shuddered as an image of my father hit me.

I immediately felt lost and hopeless. "Oh my God," I thought. "My depression is directly related to what happened here." It seems obvious, I know. But it was a revelation to me at the time.

That's what Tink did for me. She took me back, where I didn't want to go, so I could move forward.

CHRISTMAS IN FEBRUARY

Rochelle got worse and was admitted again to a county mental hospital. She lived there for a few months but then she had to move. Medicare required that she be transferred every few months—when her coverage ran out it was like they needed to hit the reset button to get the coverage started up again. And each time required a move to a different facility.

She had sustained three heart attacks over the years, caused by her diabetes as well as her drug and alcohol use. We weren't sure she was getting her three daily insulin injections because mental hospitals couldn't always provide the medical care she also required.

Renee was my one reliable sibling. She had stopped doing drugs and she was holding down a steady job. She and I would go to visit Rochelle at the different places where she lived.

At the last county hospital where Rochelle ended up, I remember the residents were screaming. The building stank of urine and some sort of sickening cleaner. Rochelle was tied down to her bed in her room. She had always been very meticulous about her grooming, just like Dad, but she was unshaven, and her furry legs were splayed on top of the sheets. The woman paid to be her sitter had cornrowed her hair for her, and she looked ridiculous, an obese white woman with tight little cornrows pulling back on her temples and accentuating the fatness of her face.

She had just been given a large dose of Haldol, a drug that I later found out can lead to cardiac arrest in heart patients, and she was delirious and sleepy. When she saw us she gave us a huge smile.

Renee and I talked with her. In front of Rochelle I told Renee that Rochelle had been the one who kept us all going during the hungry, poor years after our Dad left. "She even tried to keep Mom from hitting us sometimes by distracting her or making sure we did everything we were supposed to."

Renee looked like she couldn't believe it. I said, "No kidding. She used to get beaten maybe even more than the rest of us."

Rochelle beamed like we were giving her a compliment.

After about an hour, Rochelle started slurring her words and her eyes began drooping, but she forced herself to talk. "I remember one time. You were just born, Risé, and Mom didn't have Polio yet. We put on a play for her—Rhonda and Robert and me. I don't remember what it was about. And Mom clapped. She looked really happy. And Mom said, 'I was in a play in junior high. I thought I might be an actress.' But then it passed. And she said, 'Rochelle, change your sister's diaper.' But I was always trying to see her like that again."

She looked like she had fallen asleep for a moment. But then she said, "You, Risé, you were the one who tried hardest to make Mom like you."

What a waste of time, I thought.

Renee said, "I think you and Mom are the most alike."

I spun my head toward her to see who she was talking to. But just then Rochelle sat straight up in the bed. "Quiet, you two. I can hear the guy down the hall. He's lying about me." She cocked her head to the side, like my Yorkie. "Listen."

Then she broke into song as if we were suddenly living on a different day, with a different mood: Her voice warbled: "Have yourself a merry little Christmas. Let your heart be light. From now on our troubles will be out of sight."

It was President's Day, and there was nothing merry about it.

HITTING THE JACKPOT

In 1976 at the wedding of two friends, Carol and Gary, I had first met Les. He was good-looking and carefully groomed, with kind green eyes and a kind smile. We went on one date—but I wasn't too interested. I thought he was nice—the kiss of death for me when it came to men.

I didn't see him again for sixteen years, until I was forty. I was throwing a jewelry party, and Carol had asked Les to drop off Gary and their children at my house. When he did, Les's five-year-old daughter Kaitlyn also ran into the house, so Les had to come in to get her. He was graying and had a little belly, but this time I was attracted to him. Maybe, I thought, I was mature enough to handle a nice man who didn't want to hurt me.

We went out, first to the Chart House, and then again a week later to the Lighthouse in Hermosa Beach to listen to live music. We drove around a neighborhood in Torrance where all the houses decorate their homes for the holidays. After Christmas he took me on a four-day trip to Yosemite. At the historic Ahwahnee Hotel, which was made out of stone and wood and looked like it had been carved right out of the park's mountains, he told me he thought he was falling in love with me.

Les set about showing me just how much he loved me, and I told myself I deserved it. There wasn't a scary thing about him, and he wasn't insecure like Chris had been. He was a grown man with a good job, and he didn't drink much.

He was divorced and shared custody with his ex. On Valentine's Day I spent the night at his house when he had his two children staying there. He got angry when I wanted to sleep with him. "Are you kidding?" he said. "My children are in the house."

But later we went out to his Jeep and, as it turned out, that one time was enough to get me pregnant. It was my fourth pregnancy. But there were plenty of complications. One, I was on disability from having hurt my back at work so I didn't have the money I needed to raise a child. Two, if I were back at work I wouldn't be raising my own child but instead working to pay someone else to do it. And three, the most important one, was that Les had strong feelings.

He said, "I've done it already."

"But I haven't."

"I know, but I don't want to go through that all over again. I'm too old."

"What about me?"

"What about you? I'm not forcing you to do anything or not do anything. But you would be forcing me to have another child when I don't want to."

It was a deal breaker for us, I could see. And now that I had at last found my nice man, I didn't want to mess things up, even though it was my last chance to be a mother. I decided to get another abortion. But it was Les I never forgave for my decision.

I didn't forgive him, but I overlooked the issue and over time, I opened up to him emotionally, and told him everything about my past. He listened with compassion, focusing his pale green eyes at me. When I told him I didn't even have a high school degree, he didn't blink. "So what?" he said. "I love you, the person you are now. A high school degree wouldn't make me love you more."

No, but it might have made me love me more, I thought.

He told me I could do anything I set my mind to. He showed up for our awful family gatherings at Christmas and tolerated the fights and alcohol consumption, the stupid things my siblings would say, and the general squalor of whatever home we had gathered in.

Les would get up to pull back my chair when dinner was over, and my mother would say, "Well, she sure hit the jackpot with you."

Les would look her square in the eyes and say, in his calmest, kindest voice, "We both knew enough to find one another."

I tried to shock him, unveiling one horrible story after another. But Les just took it all with calmness. I told him about being raped in Las Vegas, and he held my hand and said, "That should never have happened to you. Those men were monsters and should be in jail."

He was kind to my siblings and my mother. But he always took my side, no matter what. "You were born perfect, and no matter what anyone tells you to the contrary, don't believe them."

His message was starting to sink in.

WAYFARERS

Les and I took it slow. I knew enough to be cautious. He had already been married twice. I had almost been married, and I didn't want to screw things up. We dated for more than a year and then we began living together in a place of our own. I still hoped that somehow Les might relent and I might be able to get pregnant.

During the occasional weeks when his children stayed with us, I got to test out my parenting skills. I worked extra hard to be attentive but not pushy, fun and kind but not a pushover. I made sure we had treats and healthy meals for the kids. I suggested game nights and movie nights. It was exhausting to be so careful, but I was terrified of messing things up and proving myself to be an awful parent.

It didn't seem to matter what I did anyway. His kids, Kaitlyn and Ryan, were respectful and friendly but they never really needed anything from me. When after eight years Les and I finally decided to get married, they were unsurprised, supportive, helpful, and unexcited.

I set about planning the perfect wedding, one appropriate for my age and one that our friends would enjoy. Les and I settled on the Wayfarers Chapel as our venue. A glass and wood structure designed by Frank Lloyd Wright, the Chapel was perched on the bluffs of Palos Verdes, overlooking Catalina Island, nestled among Redwoods.

Between the two of us we had a small army of friends, and we invited them all to the event. Tink officiated the ceremony. She had spent months writing it, and she got it just right. My brother Raymond walked me down the aisle. Our first dance was to Etta James's "At Last."

As Les put the ring on my finger I looked out at our guests and thought that all the friendly faces gathered there for us on the edge of the Pacific on a stellar day is what success and happiness looked like.

CHEATING

After leaving Sealy, I worked at several other places, but I always wanted to be a realtor. Working for a mattress company had made sense for me, a person who, while growing up, had always had to share a bed. Real estate was the next logical step: I had never felt my family was safe. At any moment we might have to move. I wanted to focus on helping people have what I hadn't had. I liked the feeling of matching people with the perfect home, one they could own and live in forever.

Once I earned my real estate license, I went to work as an agent for RE/MAX.

One day Raymond called to tell me his wife Laura had cheated on him. He was broken up, crying, unsure what to do. Les decided the four of us should fly to Hawaii—maybe a vacation was what everyone needed.

But Laura's boyfriend showed up in Hawaii too, making it clear their marriage was done. So then we took Raymond to Costa Rica to recover from the vacation we had taken him on to get over the cheating.

In Costa Rica I counseled Raymond on real estate, and he decided to sell his house in Temecula. I helped him, managing the sale for him that summer, even though Temecula was pretty far from where Les and I lived. On open house days, I would drive the two hours southeast from L.A., past ranches and avocado farms and vineyards, listening to a golden oldies station, the AC blasting against the oppressive heat. When I'd finally arrive in Temecula, I'd buy some flowers and a Nestle Toll House cookies package at a local grocery store. My dress would be wrinkled from the hot car. But I'd smooth it out and freshen up in Raymond's bathroom, putting the flowers in a little vase and lighting lavender candles I'd brought. I'd bake the cookies to make his house smell good and set out my business cards, sell sheets, and sign-up forms on the dining room table.

I ended up making the drive about six times, for two open houses and four private showings, and then we had our buyer. Raymond was relieved, and I was glad to be free from the long drive. I told him to let me know when he was ready to buy and we'd find him the perfect place.

That Christmas, I was making individual calendars for everyone in my family. The phone rang, and I stepped away from my computer to answer it. It was my assistant. She said, "Risé, did your brother buy a new house?"

"No. I'm just waiting for him to tell me he's ready, and then we're going to go looking."

"Well, there was a listing I just came across. I'd been following the property, and I see that a Raymond Myers just bought it."

I hung up the phone, furious. After everything we'd done for Raymond, he had gone out and found himself his own place, depriving me of a commission. I called him to confront him, and he made up a lame excuse about how he hadn't wanted to burden me. In the mail a few days later I got a check from him for $1,100. I tore it up.

EMPTY WELL

One day I was on my way to work. It was 7 a.m. My phone rang. I couldn't understand what the caller was saying.

It sounded like "I fresh senespen slarfor."

"What?"

"Sparser need to horgel."

It was Rhonda. I knew that voice even if I couldn't understand it.

When Rochelle started doing drugs again, her husband joined AA and left her. She moved in with Rhonda for a while. One day Rochelle had called me and asked for help.

"It was harder on me than the rest of you," she wailed into the phone. "That's why I drink. I need it to survive. How am I going to stop?"

I asked a friend to help get Rochelle into the hospital over the weekend. Then I found her a thirty-day treatment program and paid for it.

Rochelle stayed for a week and then went back to Rhonda's.

About a year later Rochelle asked me for help again. Again I got her into a program, Serenity House, with twelve other addicts in recovery. I paid for that too, and Rochelle stayed for six months but never got sober. Instead, she would drive over to my house every day and let herself in while I was gone at work. She would stay and watch TV and then go back to Recovery House at night before I got home. I knew because she would get the timing wrong and I would see her car in my driveway after work. I'd turn around and leave so I wouldn't have to deal with her and listen to her talk about how she had been treated more unfairly than the rest of us.

In some ways it was rougher for her, I knew. But I wasn't sure that it was my responsibility to make things better for her, especially when she wasn't willing to participate.

I had paid to send Robert to rehab too. He had gone through the program and then started drinking again, right after.

Now Rhonda was calling, and I was sure she was calling for help.

"I have to go," I said and hung up. Then I burst into tears. Just the sound of her slurred plea was enough to trigger it. I loved helping people. It made me feel valued and loveable, the feelings I'd been hunting down my whole life. I spent huge amounts of time and money doing things for my friends. But I couldn't keep helping when the help wasn't helpful. I didn't want to get any more calls like that. I didn't want to spit into a desert. After a few minutes of feeling sorry for myself, I gritted my teeth and made the decision.

I said, "That's it. No more."

A therapist I saw once told me my mother was a dry well.

"You can't get water out. It's empty."

"But," I tried to argue.

"No buts. It's a matter of physics," she said. And then very slowly she added, "There-is-no-water."

My mother the empty well. My father the flash flood.

In her later years, I had stopped visiting my mother much. I lived in Redondo Beach, and she was in Torrance, an easy drive for me. The few times I did visit her, sometimes she'd be a good listener, and sometimes she'd say horrible things to me. I had to recognize that her fury and meanness were not caused by her addiction.

Just as important, I got that I could never get what I was looking for, the feeling of being valued and loved.

One Mother's Day, I spent hours preparing a home for listing, weeding the garden, scrubbing the bathroom, scouring the kitchen sink, all for people I hadn't even met yet, just potential future clients. In honor of Mother's Day, I worked on a home for strangers. I didn't go visit Mom that day.

I had taken my share of abuse. But when I got to the point where I was done, I never changed my mind.

EMPTY BED

Les and I traveled. We attended tennis tournaments. We went whale watching and skiing. His kids graduated and left home but came by once a week for Taco Tuesday. We went to see our favorite performers in concert. We threw costume parties and holiday parties.

We hardly ever fought. From the outside we looked like the perfect couple.

We had been married for four years when Les stopped wanting to have sex. Here was one of the few men I had slept with sober, a tick off my to-do list, and now this man didn't want to have sex with me. How was it that I, victim of multiple rapes and molestations, could have ended up with a man who just wasn't interested?

I thought about Al and now I understood better the deal he had made with Marge. But I didn't want to do that. I wanted Les to want me.

I would climb on top of him and nothing.

I would put my foot on his lap and he would lift it up and put it down.

I would reach over at the movie theater and he would gently swat my hand away.

"Is it me?" I asked, quite reasonably.

"No. You're gorgeous."

"Well then what is it?"

"I'm just not in the mood."

"You're never in the mood."

On vacations to exotic, steamy, tropical locales, I got Viagra for him, and he wouldn't take it.

One time, when I pleaded for him to come to bed, he barked, "It's all about sex with you." He started complaining about our soft mattress after that, and eventually moved into another room.

I grew lonely. On Christmas Day of 2010, I was sitting on our couch, wrapped in blankets. Images flashed across the screen of the TV.

I was in my own house surrounded by things Les and

I had bought, nice things. No one was screaming or hitting anyone. There was no baby with a diaper that needed changing, no mother needing a drink refill. I had gone from a house full of people, noise, bad smells, and no space to a place where I was all alone amid stillness, lavender candles, and an empty couch—from a place with no boundaries to a place with boundaries I wanted to be crossed. I called to Les to come watch a movie with me. He said he had work to do and walked away.

I had everything I had worked for. But, as it turned out, it wasn't what I really needed.

That day I told Les I was leaving. He listened carefully and said, "Okay," which was a disappointment since I had hoped he would fight back. Then, even more infuriatingly, he asked calmly if we could wait a year to divorce for financial reasons. I refused to be provoked into a show of anger by his ultraplacid manner. So I agreed. Then he said, "You won't make it without me."

That one finally got to me. I slapped the table with my hand and said, "Really?" I liked a challenge.

REAL ESTATE

I got to work. I started cleaning out our house, going through everything to separate what was mine from what was his. We paid off all our debts. I took my time, carefully packing up my stuff.

I also threw myself into work. The first thing I needed to do was learn more, so I started by reaching out to Sue, the manager and top producer at our RE/Max office. She invited me to go walking with her every day.

"Great," I said.

"Meet me at five tomorrow morning."

My heart sank. Every evening I prayed for rain and every morning I cursed the alarm, but I still made myself get up and put on my workout clothes. I listened carefully to my friend during our walks, and then when I got back home I wrote down everything she had said so I wouldn't forget it.

I implemented all her recommended strategies, focusing at least fifty percent of my time on marketing and cementing my client base, getting more involved in professional organizations, tracking data about my sales and performance, and signing up for workshops and seminars. I set weekly, monthly, and annual goals. As I drove to each new listing, I would blast Cher's "You Haven't Seen the Last of Me."

In spite of or maybe partly because of Les's negative assessment of my chances of survival without him, I made $350,000 the year of our separation.

Over the next decade I went on to hit all the high points in my career. In 2013, I received the Platinum Club Award, and in 2014, the RE/MAX Lifetime Hall of Fame Award. I was on the cover of *Executive Agent Magazine*, which is like the *Rolling Stone* of the realtor world.

I made over $1 million in real estate sales. Three times I was the featured realtor on HGTV's "House Hunters," a real estate-focused reality show.

Clients wrote me fan mail. I sold houses to several well-known professional athletes, my Facebook page was full and current and thriving. I became Executive Director for networking for a Los Angeles area RE/MAX.

I looked for ways to give back. I spoke at women's recovery homes and at Skid Row AA meetings. Yearly I collected coats for the homeless living in McArthur Park in Los Angeles.

With friends, I became the go-to person when any of them needed help. I also celebrated my friends by putting on birthday parties and baby showers.

I had made it to the top, achieving everything I wanted. But the minute I reached my goals, it was like I had moved the finish line over to a different track.

I loved making my clients happy, finding them the best place to make their home. I loved donating money and time to good causes. I loved my friends and my home. But something was missing.

I was scared. For so long my desire to "make it" had kept me going. Now what?

One day I drove along the coast on Highway 101. The Santa Anas were blowing, and I felt restless. I stopped at a pullout and leaned against my car to stare over the ocean at the horizon. I watched a group of seagulls fighting over something on a rock down below. My family, I thought.

I realized I was looking for some new real estate, of a different nature, a new place to claim.

How was it possible that I had transformed my life so

much, from my my earliest days at the end of a boot or a fist, hungry and living in squalor, that I had found a way to stop drinking, which was the only thing that had kept me going through all those years, and yet here I was feeling dissatisfied?

How dare I hope for anything more? And yet I did. Maybe that was the miracle people had been telling me to look for.

THREE DEATHS

One thing I learned was that being sober didn't mean that life got easier. It just meant I would be awake enough to feel it, good or bad. About twenty years after Dad died and just one after I left Les, Tink called from Michigan, where she had her summer lake house, and told me she had cancer. My heart fell a foot.

"It's all the rage," she joked.

"But—what will happen?" I blurted.

"Honey, we'll find out. Listen, I'm going to stay on longer here to be near my family while I deal with the chemo."

"No. I'll miss you too much."

"I'll miss you more."

I thought about her constantly, worrying, but my worries about Tink were interrupted soon after. I got a call from Renee who, with her son, had just moved in with my Mom. Because of her drug use Renee had lost custody of Trevor, but when she had gotten sober he had come back to live with her again.

"Mom's in the hospital," she said. She told me that she had already left to go to work, but when Trevor woke up to go to school, he found Mom lying on the floor of the bathroom. She had fallen and hit her head. Trevor called Renee, and she called 911.

I went to the hospital, and Mom was lying in a bed, sort of alert but sort of not. There was something missing from her eyes, like a fire had been blown out. For a week, she fell in and out of a coma, sometimes mumbling, sometimes saying things like, "Who brought the flowers?" or "Is everybody here?" We all took turns staying with her at the hospital, watching her fade out.

She didn't look elegant or classy. She looked small and withered, and her head was slumped, her weak neck compressed against the pillow. Her nails, once covered with acrylics, shiny and dagger sharp, were cracked and chipped. I held her hand and thought about all the times it had been raised against me.

Renee said, "Well, Mom loves to sleep, and this is like the Grand Prize."

When she lapsed into a coma for good, we made the decision to stop feeding her.

At her memorial, Renee told me that Mom had once told her I was the one who had hurt her the most.

"What?"

"That's what she said."

"But that doesn't make any sense."

"I think it's because you needed her the least."

"So is that why she always acted like she needed me to do a million things for her?"

Renee shrugged.

Weeks later in Mom's possessions I found an index card she had written about me as part of the AA program step of making amends. The card read,

> *Risé*
> *Harm: her childhood was lacking*
> *enough attention, love and creature*
> *comforts, stability, privacy, safety.*
> *failed to protect her from sibling*
> *molestation failed to teach self*
> *discipline never enough money*
> *or interest in her school activities.*
> *Not emmotionally available.*
> *Seldom praised her for her cleanliness—*
> *I was not a good example.*

I later noticed that she never used a personal pronoun to show her responsibility until the very last sentence: The only thing she owned up to was not being "a good example." And even in this last message, she managed to criticize me for not learning enough self-discipline. But at the time, sadly, I felt grateful to know that Mom knew how I had suffered.

Just that small thing.

I had a dream the night of her memorial that God had written Mom a letter congratulating her on changing more than most people ever do.

In the morning, I drove to Palm Springs and hiked in the canyons for three days. In my journal I wrote this:

> I have a new level of trust in the universe.
> Literally everything looks brighter, the grass
> is greener, the sky is bluer. I feel more alive
> than I have in years. And even though it
> has been painful, at the same time, it's been
> wonderful. I believe this is the last gift my
> mother gave me.

There hadn't been many gifts, and this one came with an aftertaste.

After Mom's memorial and my visit to Palm Springs, I flew to Michigan to see Tink. That's when I found out she had taken a turn for the worse, much worse, and her sister Connie was staying in the lake house with her to care for her. True to her character, Tink hadn't called to tell me because she knew I was dealing with my Mom's death, and she didn't want to be a burden. The chemo had made her puffy, and she seemed almost lost in her body, but she fixed her eyes on me and saw everything. She weakly squeezed my hand when I talked to her about my Mom's memorial.

It became clear to me in that first hour that no one expected her to recover, and I selfishly cried for my loss— my losses—alone in the room Connie had set me up in. I read to Tink on those last days, whatever she wanted, books, newspapers, magazines. I hung out with her family. I selfishly talked about myself because I was desperate to get as much of her attention as possible before the end.

She was in pain. Every time she groaned, I wanted to talk to her about it, to get some answers about God and why people have to suffer. But Tink didn't have any more answers for me.

The last words she ever spoke were, "I'm getting better."

After she died, Connie and I cleaned her body and dressed her. I put a stuffed dog on her chest to keep her company.

Back home after Tink's memorial, I settled into my usual routine, selling homes, seeing friends, occasionally visiting my siblings, especially Renee. But life felt grayer, and the quiet that I had always craved was now like a yawning weight.

A few months after Tink's death, Renee and I were driving to the hospital to visit Rochelle again. We hadn't seen her since that last time when she had broken into song. It was summer, and we had the windows down to let in a breeze.

Renee decided to call ahead to let the hospital know we were coming. The receptionist said, "You're calling for Rochelle?"

"Yes."

"She's dead."

Renee explained very carefully that we wanted to see Rochelle *Myers*. But the receptionist knew exactly who she meant. "She died yesterday. She had a heart attack."

We found out later that the hospital had called Rhonda, who was listed as next of kin, but Rhonda hadn't listened to the message.

GRATITUDE SPOON

Somewhere in a magazine I read about a gratitude spoon Thanksgiving tradition. The idea was that you would pass a spoon around the table. Each person would take a turn to hold it and speak about what they were grateful for. In 2014, I decided to give my friends and clients wooden spoons engraved with the word *gratitude*.

I started the tradition among them, and I figured I might as well try it with my family too. The Thanksgiving dinner was at Renee's. Raymond was not there but Robert and Rhonda were. Henry, who had just been released from prison, was living in Renee's garage so he was there, as were Renee's sons.

I went ahead and introduced the spoon concept. It started out okay. Henry said he was grateful for the food, and he made a crack that he was hungry. Renee said she was grateful for her boys.

Then it was my turn. I said something like this: "I'm grateful to be alive, to be sober. For all of you."

But there was a lot more I could have said. Rhonda was next but she had gone to the bathroom, and while we waited for her I made a list in my head.

I was grateful for Tink and Al, of course. And at that point, Les too. I was so thankful for Renee. All of my dear friends. Reverend Shirley's teachings, the things I learned from David. The kindness of Miss Mary, and Mrs. and Mr. Kim. My AA friends and sponsors. My dogs.

Rhonda staggered back to her seat, interrupting my thoughts. She grabbed the spoon and slurred, "It's good we're all together but Mom and Rochelle aren't here. So Renee said to me once, 'Why doesn't Mom come and visit you more?' So I was like 'Well, she's fucking loaded, you know, she's just up the block but—.'"

Renee interrupted Rhonda by patting her on the back, "We know. You don't need to explain at this table."

Everybody laughed nervously and Rhonda went on: "Just thankful to be clean and sober."

Renee covered her mouth with her hand to stifle her

laugh and Rhonda didn't hear her. She just went on talking, this time about her son: "And one last thing. I don't mean to put a downer on anything but Max made the, the—."

I tried to help her out: "The three bean soup. The three bean thing."

Rhonda got out, "Green bean."

Henry confirmed, "Green bean."

Rhonda continued, "The green bean casserole that he learned from Rochelle. I'm just so grateful that Rochelle's not in pain anymore."

Then she started infusing her gratitude with sarcasm: "And I don't know why Mom and Rochelle never showed up in my dreams or anything, but every morning I kiss the ring and say good morning Rochelle good morning Mom, so thanks to all of you for being loving and supportive." Then she sat down abruptly, almost missing her chair.

I looked at the people sitting around the table—what was left of my family, and saw that the Gratitude Spoon was not going to work with them. But that was okay. It didn't need to. I could live my life for my siblings, forever stuck in the spot where they were trapped, unchanging, and throwing away my own chances just to stay stuck with them. Or I could save myself. I could save one life, my own, and make it something.

It was on that Thanksgiving that I decided, then and there, that I was done. I was free. For that I was grateful.

RISE UP

The beach is a short walk from my home. I go there and look out over the water with my back to the city my family has called home for almost sixty years. My family, the pack of characters that has weighed me down my whole life.

The coastline is, for me, a key touchstone, a visible boundary to help frame a life that got a shaky beginning.

The way it all started was in Cocoa Beach, Florida. My grandparents owned a restaurant/bar there, and their one and only fifteen-year-old daughter went to work for them as a hostess. My Dad at nineteen was stationed in Florida, and one day he walked into that very bar. He saw my pretty mother expertly managing the busy lunch crowd, her curvy figure darting around tables as she directed people to the bar, handed out menus, collected payment. She saw my handsome father in his khaki uniform with its sharp creases watching her approvingly from his stool at the bar.

They were young. Life was calling to them. No one knew what to expect.

She got pregnant with Rochelle right away. Just like that, and then sixty years later here we are.

Growing up, I didn't know what to expect either. But I kept hoping for and striving for success. I had a picture in my mind of what it would look like, and I thought it was a measurable, universal standard, like a finish line. People reached out their hands to me and I grabbed and held on so they could pull me toward it.

Most people would say I've crossed that finish line. But guess what. It doesn't exist.

Instead, I have found that we orbit around the people and experiences we need, the ones that call out to us, the ones that pull us in, for better or worse. The gravity that pulls us? It's need. It's attraction. It's the weight of heavy sorrow. We break away for other galaxies when we're ready and when we can.

Reverend Shirley taught me to take responsibility for my life. Al taught me to be ready, as life is always moving and changing. Tink taught me to see and cherish the miracle of it all. To forgive, accept, and love myself.

I've spent a lot of time mourning not having a child of my own. But, in fact, I now see that I have had a child to raise, and it's taken a lifetime to raise her, that little girl with the hard-to-pronounce name who wanted desperately to be loved.

As I look out toward the ocean from my spot on the beach, I feel love for that child.

I feel love for my family too—Mom, Dad, Rochelle, Robert, Rhonda, Raymond, Renee, Henry, and Lisa— imperfect stragglers stumbling toward and often away from the light.

And I feel a new love for something growing in my heart. What is it?

Call it hope. Trust. A desire to share what I have worked so hard for so long to learn. I don't know yet. I'm sure it will change along the way. But it will be mine to nurture and grow.

From that young girl in the photo all the way to me now, my success has been, that against all odds, I have survived and survived well. And that survival has taught me how to rise up, again and again, to see what's next.

GRATITUDE

I hesitated to do a Gratitude Page, because it could easily be as long as the book itself.

I have had the blessing of so many angels on my path, both in the physical and invisible world. I introduced you to some in this book, but there were others too – and you know who you are. Friends who have stood by me for years, and through the thick and thin of times. I am forever grateful.

To my family – we argue, we fight. We even stop talking to each other at times. The love I feel for you will always be there.

Of course, my AA sponsors and friends, who, for obvious reasons, I will not name.

Words cannot express my gratitude for Sakada. Throughout the process, her encouragement and support has been my saving grace.

I do want to give a special acknowledgement to Suzanne St. John who designed my beautiful book cover. My thanks to Pamela Boboc for her help on my website and more.

Finally, I have to give a shout out to Maddie, my dog. Maddie has been part of the writing process from the beginning, sleeping next to me as I wrote. And as I relived my childhood, she was always a welcome snuggle break from the very tough emotions that surfaced.

Risé Myers is a speaker who inspires audiences with her "ability to rise." As her memoir *Rise* reveals, her own life story has been her greatest teacher. The miracle is that she released the damaging effects of abuse and molestation, and embraced her own self-worth. The blessing is that she chose to share her experience and insight with others.

www.risemyers.com

Made in the USA
San Bernardino, CA
01 February 2018